The
Law
of
Attraction

The
Law
of
Attraction

**MASTER THE UNIVERSAL ENERGY
TO UNLEASH YOUR POTENTIAL**

MITESH KHATRI
INDU KHATRI

JAICO PUBLISHING HOUSE

Ahmedabad Bangalore Bhopal Chennai
Delhi Hyderabad Kolkata Lucknow Mumbai

Published by Jaico Publishing House
A-2 Jash Chambers, 7-A Sir Phirozshah Mehta Road
Fort, Mumbai - 400 001
jaicopub@jaicobooks.com
www.jaicobooks.com

THE LAW OF ATTRACTION
ISBN 978-81-8495-836-2

First Jaico Impression: 2016
11th Jaico Impression: 2021

Page design and layout: Inosoft Systems, Delhi

Printed by
Trinity Academy For Corporate Training Limited, Mumbai

I dedicate this book to the Universal Energy which has helped me co-create an amazing life with the help of the Law of Attraction. Thank you, Universe.

Next, I want to thank Indu, my wife and co-author, for inspiring me and supporting me to practice the Law of Attraction consistently, creating magical results in our life. Thank you, Indu. I love you.

I would like to thank my mentors Raj Mali, Sahil Surthy (Gyandev), Wayne Dyer and most importantly Dr. Sudhir Arora who taught me the Law of Attraction. Thank you, Dr. Arora for believing in Indu and me and for reviewing our book.

Thank you, Mom and Dad, for always believing in me and for teaching me to dream big.

I want to thank my publisher Akash Shah of Jaico Publishing House for believing in me and helping me manifest this book into reality.

Finally, I want to dedicate this book to you and to all my readers who are committed to learn and apply the Law of Attraction to unleash the potential within.

CONTENTS

AUTHOR'S NOTE

Thank you, dear reader, for purchasing *The Law of Attraction*. I want to personally promise you that this book can help you achieve your dreams and your goals faster than ever before with the help of the Law of Attraction.

As a token of appreciation for buying this book here are bonus gifts worth $500:

1. Free 5 audio lessons on *The Law of Attraction*.
2. Free eBook on 'How to Wake Up Early and Love It.'
3. Free eBook on 'The Power of Making Decisions Right.'
4. Free video on Emotional Intelligence.
5. Free video on Leadership Skills.
6. Free video on Decision Making Skills.
7. Free first chapter of my bestselling book *Awaken the Leader in You*.
8. Free subscription to my *Life Leadership* blog.

All you have to do is subscribe here at http://www.miteshkhatri.com/Loa-Gifts/ and I will send you the above free gifts right away.

If you like this book, please show your appreciation by leaving a positive review on Amazon or Flipkart to help many more people benefit from the Law of Attraction.

WHY READ THIS BOOK?

There are TWO good reasons to read this book.

Success and Happiness

This is the first and most important reason. I refer to them as one because I believe success and happiness complement each other.

Everybody in the world is interested in being successful and happy in every area of life.

There is a magical power hidden within you which, if harnessed, can enable you to attract success and happiness in your relationships, money, career, health and anything your heart desires. Yes, that's right, almost anything your heart desires!

This magical power is known as **The Law of Attraction.** There are many other books that have discussed the power of Law of Attraction:

- *The Secret* by Rhonda Byrne
- *Creative Visualization* by Shakti Gawain

- *The Power of Your Sub-conscious Mind* by Joseph Murphy
- *You Can Heal Your Life* by Louise Hay
- *Think and Grow Rich* by Napoleon Hill

These and other such books have proven to us that we carry within ourselves unlimited magical power to attract anything we want in our life. We are the creators of our own destiny and we have the power to be, to do and to have anything we want to.

The Law of Attraction was revealed to us by Lord Krishna in *Bhagavad Gita* centuries ago; scientists like Albert Einstein discovered it much later. We will learn more about this in the following chapters. I have been learning, practicing and teaching the Law of Attraction for more than 10 years now. And even though people are now aware of it, very few people really use this magical power.

> **Our deepest fear is not that we are inadequate; our deepest**
> **fear is that we are powerful beyond measure.**
>
> – Mariam Williamson

Not everyone is ready for the unlimited power of the Law of Attraction. However, the fact that you are reading this book means that *you* are ready for it. You have attracted this book because you want to understand and harness this magical power within you. This power belongs to you. It is time you use it.

The Second Reason

You must read this book because you need to know that you are already using the Law of Attraction unconsciously and that too possibly *against yourself.*

Yes! As you read this book you will realize that you are already using the magical power of the Law of Attraction to hurt yourself unconsciously. I know this sounds absurd, but it's true.

- The relationship problems that you may have.
- All money problems you may have.
- All the struggles you may be experiencing at work.
- All the health issues you may have.
- All the sadness you may be experiencing.
- All the career challenges that you may be facing.
- All the bad luck you might be experiencing is only because unconsciously you are using the Law of Attraction against yourself.

If what I am saying is true, it's really dangerous, isn't it?

But cheer up! If you are unconsciously using the Law of Attraction against yourself, then you are also unconsciously using it to your own advantage.

Yes! The good luck that you have in your life right now is also a result of using the Law of Attraction. So good things that are happening in your relationships, the opportunities you are attracting in your professional life, the money, the happiness that you are attracting right now in your life is a result of *you* using the Law of Attraction.

The problem is that since you are using it unconsciously, you are unable to take full advantage of the magical powers of the Law of Attraction.

There's good news though. This book will guide you to understand exactly how to use the Law of Attraction consciously to attract more of what you want and less of what you don't want.

Here is the story of a young man who learnt the Law of Attraction and consciously attracted a better job with a better salary.

Hi, my name is Lavesh Agrawal and I am a software engineer. I learnt and practiced the Law of Attraction to achieve my goal – to change my current job and get a deserving hike in salary.

I had been trying to switch my job for six months, but wasn't getting the right opportunities. I had started believing that the market was not good and that I would have to wait for at least three years in my current job to get the kind of hike I wanted.

It was then I learnt about the Law of Attraction from Mitesh. It changed my life forever. I realized that I am the source of all the attractions that are happening in my life. Mitesh taught me a way to change what I was consciously attracting.

I started using techniques like visualization, affirmations, recording affirmations, writing my goals every day and started behaving as if I had already got my dream job. As a result, I achieved my goal within a month.

YES! I attracted a job which matched my passion and also got a hike of 75% over my previous salary.

What was not happening for six months, I attracted in just one month with using the Law of Attraction consciously.

I started using the Law of Attraction in every area of my life and have achieved many more goals since then, both in my personal and professional life.

Looking at the transformation in me, even my parents and my brother learnt the Law of Attraction techniques from Mitesh and experienced extraordinary benefits in their life.

I am very grateful to Mitesh for introducing my family and me to the art of manifestation, the Law of Attraction.

You see, Lavesh consciously used the power of the Law of Attraction and attracted what he wanted. So can you.

So are you ready to understand the Law of Attraction? Are you ready to learn how to consciously attract what you want? I hear you saying YES! Ok then, let's go to the next chapter to understand what the Law of Attraction is…

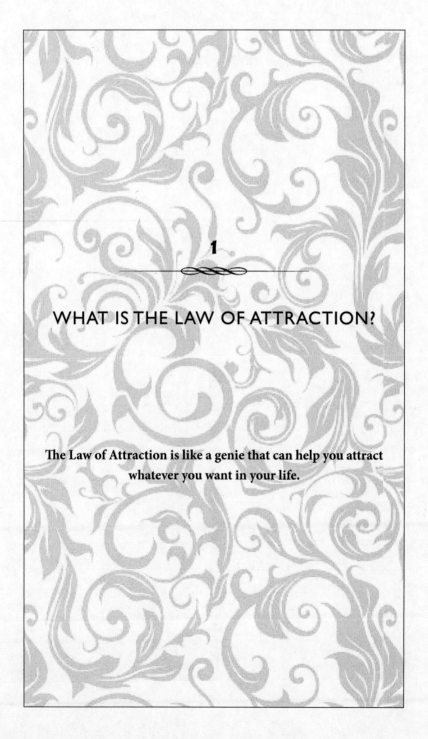

1

WHAT IS THE LAW OF ATTRACTION?

The Law of Attraction is like a genie that can help you attract
whatever you want in your life.

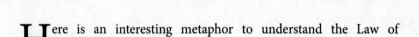

H ere is an interesting metaphor to understand the Law of Attraction.

Imagine having access to a personal genie who would fulfil every wish you had.

I am sure you would love to gain access to such a personal genie. Well, your wish is about to come true. This book will give you access to your personal genie who will grant you anything you desire.

But where is this genie? Where is he hidden? Let's find out from a small story.

This story is about a genie who had magical powers to fulfil unlimited wishes for his master. God wanted to hide this genie from people who would misuse it, but make it accessible to good people who would use the genie for a good cause.

Now God was really confused about where to hide this powerful genie. After thinking for a long time, God finally found a place where the wrong people would never find the genie, only the good ones would.

So God hid this powerful genie *inside* human beings!

God was sure that most people are so busy looking for success and happiness on the outside that they would never look within themselves.

So the amazing fact is that your personal genie is not hidden in a lamp but within you – called the Law of Attraction.

To take control of your destiny, you must take control of the genie inside you.

In my own case, I dedicate my success to this personal genie – the Law of Attraction. If it wasn't for the Law of Attraction, I would probably still be struggling.

After I learnt about the genie, I realized that I had been using it against myself.

Financially, I was attracting failure in my business no matter how hard I worked. I was attracting bad relationships which left me with a heavy heart every time. My health also suffered. I was an ordinary person with extraordinary dreams.

This was my condition until 2003.

In 2003, I hit rock bottom in every area of my life and didn't think it could get any worse than that. This was the time I started using the Law of Attraction. I had read about it in 1997, but at the time it seemed too good to be true and too esoteric, so I never felt the urge to use it.

Later in 2003, after facing many failures, I needed some good luck to change my life. I was at a stage where anything that gave me hope was good enough for me.

So the first time I used my genie, the Law of Attraction, I asked for a beautiful life partner who would love me, accept me the way I am and support me in my hard times.

To cut the long story short, I attracted my life partner, my wife Indu, in just a week after I used my genie consciously for the first time. Can you believe that? Just a week! That was awesome. Here's how it happened…

I was attending a workshop called 'Mind Control' by Dr. Sudhir Arora, one of my mentors in Pune. There I saw this beautiful woman whose name was Indu. We were introduced during the workshop and instantly became friends. A week after that, I called her out for a party; she accepted immediately. That evening, even though we were amongst a lot of people in the party, it seemed as if we were alone because we were in one corner talking to each other endlessly. The world around us did not exist; it was just the two of us. Our connection was magical!

The next day she invited me for coffee at her place in the evening. Our coffee session, which started at 7 PM, extended to dinner, then to late night coffee, and eventually, we went on talking till 5 AM. That morning we accepted that we had something special between us. She said she loved me, I kissed her, and that was the beginning of a long life partnership between us.

Indu and I got married a year after that, on February 16, 2005 and we have been happily married ever since. In fact, anybody who meets us cannot ignore the love and chemistry we share and we always get compliments for being a beautiful couple. Here is a photo of me and my sweetheart Indu…

This was only the beginning of magic in our life.

If you understand and use the Law of Attraction correctly, you can manifest anything you want.

I taught the Law of Attraction to Indu and we started using it together. Together we asked our genie to help us attract success in our corporate training business.

We started using the Law of Attraction every single day and saw magic every day in our life. Our company has shown a 100 per cent growth ratio almost every year. Even when other companies were struggling to survive, we grew stronger and bigger.

I have attracted a dream life…

Today I work for only 15 days a month and spend the rest of the month with my family having fun, reading books, watching movies and enjoying life.

I have the privilege and opportunity to train thousands of senior executives every year in more than 200 multinational companies and coach some of the topmost leaders of the corporate world. I am an international bestselling author. I travel to different countries conducting workshops and making a difference in people's lives. I get to participate in adventurous activities like making people walk on fire and go on 5-Star holidays every three months with family and friends. Most importantly, I have learnt how to manifest anything I want using the Law of Attraction.

Now I am not sharing all this with you to impress you but to show you the kind of magic that is possible with the Law of Attraction.

Anything you wish for is possible, provided you know how to attract it.

Indu and I still feel overwhelmed with the kind of magic we experience every day in our life.

Now you too have access to the same genie, the same Law of Attraction.

In this book, I will share with you everything we know about the Law of Attraction so that you can also use your personal genie (the Law of Attraction) to attract the life of your dreams and all the success and happiness you deserve.

Manifestation

The Law of Attraction is also known as the process of manifestation.

What is manifestation?

When you successfully attract your goal, it is called manifestation.

For example, if you have a goal of earning $1000 and have successfully done so, in the Law of Attraction language, we will call it *manifestation complete* or *your goal of $1000 has manifested*.

Thus the Law of Attraction is also called the process of manifestation.

In simple language, when you are able to attract something, it means you have manifested it. So being a master at using the Law of Attraction means being a master at manifestation.

Everyone in the world is already using the Law of Attraction and manifesting something all the time. But most people are *unconscious* of the fact that they manifest (attract) everything that happens in their life, whether positive or negative.

Through this book you will learn how to consciously manifest your goals and attract abundance of health, wealth and happiness.

When we meet participants after our Law of Attraction workshop, we always ask, "Are you doing your daily manifestation?"

What this means is whether you are using the Law of Attraction to manifest what you want consciously.

Whenever I attract something negative in my life, I remember to ask myself how I manifested it. In other words, how did I unconsciously use the Law of Attraction and manifest negativity?

If I ever say something negative like, "I think I am going to be late today", Indu always asks me, "What are you manifesting?"

When I say something negative, I unconsciously manifest (attract) it in my life.

Remember that whenever I use the word 'manifestation' in this book, I am referring to using the Law of Attraction.

For example, if I ask you, "Are you doing you daily manifestation?" what I want to know is whether you are consciously using the Law of Attraction to attract what you want.

If you have already attracted something wrong in your life, I may ask,

"How did you manifest it?" What I want to know is how you attracted it in your life.

In order for you to use the Law of Attraction consciously and become a master of manifestation, you must know the answer to these questions:

- Why does the Law of Attraction work? What is the science behind this phenomenon?
- What are the laws that control the Law of Attraction?

If you are ready to create miracles in life and manifest your dreams, let's go to the next chapter to get the answers to the above questions.

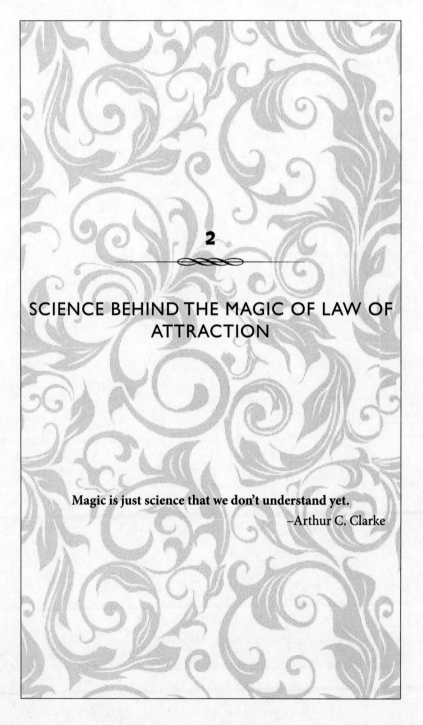

2

SCIENCE BEHIND THE MAGIC OF LAW OF ATTRACTION

Magic is just science that we don't understand yet.

–Arthur C. Clarke

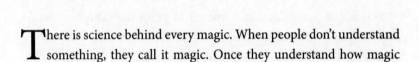

There is science behind every magic. When people don't understand something, they call it magic. Once they understand how magic works, they call it science. Here are a few examples.

In ancient times, anyone who had medical knowledge was known as a magician because people did not understand the science of medicines.

A few decades ago if I told you that you could have a mobile phone in your hands which you could carry anywhere and make calls to any part of the world, you would have called it magic.

About 20 years ago, people thought touch technology was a myth because they did not understand the science behind it. Today it is in your hands as touch phones or smartphones.

If I told you that a few years from now you would be able to download data straight in your brain, you would call it myth or magic. Once somebody understands how it works, it's called science.

Yesterday's magic is today's science and today's magic is tomorrow's science.

Once you understand how the Law of Attraction works, you will realize that this too is science, not magic. Lord Krishna speaks of this in *Bhagavad Gita*, written centuries ago, and we have even studied about it in school physics, but we have never understood what it really means.

I will first reveal to you the exact science that makes the Law of Attraction work as per physics and then we shall also understand how Lord Krishna had explained the same science in *Bhagavad Gita* according to my understanding.

Here is a story of a participant who learnt the science behind the Law of Attraction and manifested a US visa.

My name is Rahul Tapadia. I wanted to go to the United States of America to pursue Masters in Science (MS), but my visa was rejected.

I had lost all hope because I was told that since I already had a rejection by the US embassy, it was almost impossible to get a visa.

Then I learnt about the Law of Attraction from Mitesh and was surprised to learn how scientific this phenomenon is.

I applied all the techniques from this book and as a result I attracted the miracle of getting a US visa in my second attempt. In fact, I am right now in the USA as I write this letter. Not only did I manifest the visa, I also secured admission in the university I wanted.

The Law of Attraction has become a part of my lifestyle. Not only do I continue to practice it every day, but also recommend this book to my family and friends.

Thank you Mitesh, for teaching me the Law of Attraction. I would have never made it this far without practicing this science.

Here is the science that makes the Law of Attraction work.

Law of Attraction – The Science

You will be surprised to know that you were introduced to the science behind the Law of Attraction in school physics.

Now don't get worried about having to read physics. I have simplified it here for you. Once you understand how it works, you will have the conviction to use the techniques and become a master of manifestation. So here we go…

In physics, we learnt that everything around us that has mass and volume, including our body is called 'matter'. Anything that you can perceive through your five senses is called matter. Thus our world is described as 'materialistic' because everything is matter.

The clothes you wear constitute matter, the air you breathe is also matter, as are the goals you want to achieve, the people around you – everything living and non-living that has space and volume is called matter. If we look through a microscope at any piece of matter, we see that it is made of many things like atoms, molecules, neutrons, and protons. At the deepest level, there is *energy*.

Thus the formula we learnt in school was:

$$E = mc^2$$

Each one of us and everything you see around is made of energy. Water, air, all type of gases, light, mountains, trees, the furniture around you, everything that is matter is made of energy.

All the desires you have – house, car, money, relationships – anything that you want is also matter which is essentially made of energy. You are energy, I am energy, our goals are energy; everything is energy.

Remember this…

Everything is energy!

Now here is a tricky question:

If you and I are made of energy, then are we made of different energy or the same energy?

It may seem that we are separate individuals and therefore made of different energies.

Actually I am made of the very same energy that you are.

Science has proven that in the entire universe there is one singular energy, so the bottom line is that you and I are made of the same energy and thus at the energy level we are all connected as one, connected with an invisible thread of energy to one another.

But if we are connected, why can't we see the connection?

Well, we can't see it because we don't have the capacity to see energy with our naked eyes. We cannot see our bones with our naked eyes, but we can see it through an X-Ray machine. Similarly, we can't see the 'energy' connection among us. However, science has now developed the technology to not only see, but even measure the energy that we are all made of.

Just because you don't have the capacity to see something, it doesn't mean it does not exist.

I am sure you have read or heard in religious books that if you want to find God, look within yourself because God resides within you. This is not just philosophical; it also has a scientific basis to it.

God is also a form of energy and since there is a single force of energy in the universe, we have inside us the same energy that God is made of. Therefore, it is correct to say that God resides inside us.

This is why spiritual people are against violence because they know that whether you are hurting an animal or another human being, at the level of energy you are only hurting yourself or hurting the energy of God itself since everyone is made of the same energy as God.

When you are angry with someone else, why do you feel upset? Because at the level of energy, when you are angry with someone else you are also angry with yourself. That is why forgiveness is very important because by forgiving others you only forgive yourself.

You must have also heard what you give is what you get. If you give money you get more of it, if you give love you get more of it. Similarly, if you give anger you get more of it, if you give negativity you get more of it. This principle works because at the energy level what we do to others affects us as well.

Here are the Laws of Energy that control the Law of Attraction

Laws of Energy

Our universe is governed by certain laws of energy; master the laws and you master the universe.

1. Energy can neither be created nor destroyed; it can only be transformed from one form to another.

This means that all matter which is made of energy, for example a plastic bottle, can never be really created or destroyed; it can only be transformed from one form to another.

Right now the plastic bottle is in the solid form, if we heat the bottle and melt the plastic, it transforms into liquid form. Thus we have only succeeded in changing the form of energy; we did not, and cannot, destroy or create it.

Now you may be wondering, why are we learning about these laws of energy again? Understanding these laws will help you understand how to use the magical powers of the Law of Attraction.

2. The total amount of energy in the universe is always constant.

This means that no matter how much energy we use and no matter how much we transform it into different forms, the total amount of energy is always constant.

Physics also proves that...

3. Everything is made of the same energy.

We and our goals are made of the same energy; the only thing that separates us from each other is the frequency at which we vibrate. We are all one, connected at the level of energy.

Here is a scientific military experiment which proves that we are all connected at the level of energy.

Scientists took some DNA sample from a person's mouth and placed it in a device which could detect changes happening in the DNA. They put this person and his DNA sample in completely different rooms. They then showed him some pictures that made him feel a variety of emotions like happiness, sadness, irritation, excitement, etc.

The scientists were shocked to see that while the person in one room was going through emotional ups and downs, his DNA registered the same ups and downs at the exact same time in another room.

Noticing this, the scientists were shocked at this and decided to take the experiment to the next level.

What shocked the scientists most was that his DNA registered the same changes even when the person was in a completely different city. Many such scientific experiments prove that we are all connected at the level of energy.

This gets very interesting! The next law of energy tells us how to use the Law of Attraction to manifest what we want in our life.

4. Energy with the same frequency will attract each other which means 'like attracts like'.

All energy vibrates at a certain frequency and when the energy of two things vibrates at the same frequency it will attract each other like magnets. This is the Law of Attraction: *Like attracts like!*

Since our goals are made of energy, we can use this Law of Attraction to attract them towards us. In the next chapter you will learn how the Law of Attraction is already working in your life and attracting all that you already have in your life.

Let us see how these laws of energy were introduced to us by Lord Krishna in the *Bhagavad Gita*. I think of Krishna as a master of physics.

Note: **I do not claim to be a master of the *Bhagavad Gita*. This is my interpretation of the connection I find in it with the Law of Attraction.**

The Law of Attraction & The *Bhagavad Gita*

> **The soul can never be cut to pieces by any weapon, nor burned by any fire, nor moistened by water, nor withered by the wind.**
> – Bhagavad Gita

In simple words, here is how I found the connection between the Law of Attraction and the *Bhagavad Gita*:

1. What takes birth and dies is only your body, the real you which is your soul (energy or spirit) can be neither created nor destroyed, it can only change form from one life to another.

This is exactly what physics says: *Energy can be neither created nor destroyed; it can only be transformed from one form to another.*

I was quite amazed to discover this connection between *Bhagavad Gita* and the laws of energy explained in physics.

Lord Krishna knew these things centuries before science had the means to understand it. It gets even more exciting.

2. Nothing ever dies nor takes birth, everything always exists.

Physics says that the total amount of energy in the universe is always constant. So there is nothing ever lost or wasted in this life. Wow! It is as if Krishna was explaining physics.

I was most excited by the following connection:

3. God is inside everyone, if you truly want to seek God then seek within yourself.

Physics says, *everything is made of the same energy.*

If God is energy, I am also energy and we are all made of the same energy, then it makes sense that God is within all of us; it makes sense that God is in everything because everything is made of the same energy.

Isn't this connection between religion and science beautiful! I can't explain to you the excitement I feel even as I write this, as though I have found the bridge between science and religion.

In fact one of the other things said in the *Bhagavad Gita* is that the whole materialistic world is an illusion or what Krishna called '*Maya*'. Maya means illusion.

Krishna says that the world we perceive is maya or illusion because we as human beings cannot see energy, we can only see matter or the materialistic reality.

Just when I thought this was the only connection, I discovered the Law of Attraction as I think it is explained in the *Bhagavad Gita*.

4. Your Destiny will always depend on your karma.

Your actions have energy with a certain frequency; as per the law of energy, like attracts like so your actions will attract results of the same frequency.

To me, this implies that your destiny depends on your karma. So translated into the language of the Law of Attraction, your destiny will depend on the frequency of your karma.

I see this as scientific validation for what was originally set forth in the *Bhagavad Gita*. In spirituality, frequency is called consciousness. When we say we vibrate at a different frequency, spiritual people say that we are all at a different level of consciousness.

So you see, the Law of Attraction is not some positive thinking philosophy that can be taken lightly; it is based on scientific facts and works with laws which have existed for centuries.

Everything is energy and that's all there is to it. Match the frequency of the reality you want and you cannot help but get that reality. This is not just philosophy, but it's physics.

Let us put these ideas together in this question answer format to understand it better:

What is God?
God is the infinite source of energy that we are all made of.

Where is God/energy?
God/energy is everywhere, in everything and everybody including me.

Who am I?
I am energy. There is God in me.

What did the *Bhagavad Gita* mean by saying '*everything is maya*' or illusion?

What our senses show us is only the illusion of the solid matter or material; the real energy or the soul is never visible to the unseeing eye. Thus we live in a world of sensory reality or illusions (maya).

Who is everyone around me?

Everyone is God/energy which is me, so we are all ONE; only our form is different.

Why do I feel bad when I hurt someone?

Because at the level of energy, by hurting another, I hurt the self.

Why do I feel good when I love and make someone happy?

Because at the energy level, by loving another, I love myself.

Why is forgiveness important?

At the level of energy, by forgiving another person, it is the self that I forgive.

What do I deserve?

I deserve everyone and everything as they all are me – the same energy.

Can I control my destiny?

Yes. I can make my own destiny by controlling the frequency at which I vibrate.

These answers are exciting because in the course of this exploration, my best realization was that God resides in everything, including me as a scientific fact.

And now that I know I have the energy of God within me, I also know I have the power to achieve whatever I want.

Whatever I want to attract is also me at the energy level, so I deserve everything in my life because everything is in me and I am in everything.

After learning this, my perspective towards everything changed completely. I saw myself in my family, in my friends, in my colleagues, in my clients, in my problems, in all animals, in my laptop, everything around me. As a result, my respect and love for everything around me grew exponentially. I was able to empathize with people to whom I could not relate earlier because I realized that they are a part of me as I am also a part of them.

> **One should not show disrespect to any person. In reality it would be tantamount to disrespecting his own self, as the whole world is God itself.**
>
> – Bhagavad Gita

I realized why spiritual gurus like Buddha were able to unconditionally love everyone and everything around them. I realized why great leaders like Mahatma Gandhi and Nelson Mandela were against violence and wanted to win people with love.

All these great leaders knew that by hating someone else they would only hate themselves; by loving and forgiving others, they would love and forgive themselves.

What I learnt transformed me and my life forever.

In the next chapter we will explore in depth the Law of Attraction and understand how to use it. Before that, here is a small exercise for you: write down your own realization after reading about the Law of Attraction.

Summary of the Science behind the Law of Attraction

The Law of Attraction as per Physics

- Everything is made of matter, thus we call our world the 'materialistic' world.

- All matter is made of energy.
- There is only one energy in the universe, we are all made of the same energy.
- Thus, at the energy level, we are all connected, we are all one.
- You cannot see energy because of the limitations of our senses.
- God is also a form of energy and since there is only one energy in. the universe, we and God are made of the same energy.
- What we do to others affects us because we are all one at the basic energy level.

Laws of Energy

- Energy cannot be created or destroyed; it can only be transformed from one form to another.
- Thus the total amount of energy in the universe is always constant.
- All matter is made of the same energy.
- Energy is always vibrating at a certain frequency.
- Human beings cannot see, hear or feel frequencies beyond a certain point.
- Energy with the same frequency will attract each other – like attracts like.

3

LIKE ATTRACTS LIKE

What you think you become, what you feel you attract, what
you imagine you create.

–Buddha

To start with, here is the story of a dear friend and participant, Shweta Kajale, who attracted her dream car by understanding and practicing the Law of Attraction.

I had been yearning to buy a particular car for more than six months but I thought I could never afford it.

After attending the Law of Attraction workshop I realized that miracles do happen; I had to consciously manifest what I wanted.

So I started visualizing and using affirmation techniques to attract my dream car. I even used to visit car showrooms for test drives, took pictures of me sitting in the car and slowly my fears and doubts regarding not affording the car started dissolving.

Within six months after that I had saved enough money to afford the car I always wanted. Not only that, soon after that I even bought a second car and paid off both the car loans in just a year.

In fact, I was the youngest employee in my organization to achieve so much success so fast and my boss was so proud of me that he kept telling my story to everyone.

I believe I attracted the business opportunities and the money to achieve all my goals because I used the Law of Attraction to vibrate at the right frequency, by taking control of my feelings, thoughts, beliefs and actions.

Now I practice techniques like visualization, affirmation and gratitude on a daily basis and get phenomenal results, much faster than most people do in their life.

Even when I go shopping, if I can't find what I want, I close my eyes and manifest that I have found the perfect outfit I wanted. Sometimes I find exactly what I wanted and sometimes I find things which exceed my expectations.

Thank you, Mitesh, for introducing me to this wonderful law, the Law of Attractions.

Shweta Kajale
Interior designer

I hope you are encouraged by Shweta's story and are ready to create one of your own such miracle stories.

Now that you understand the science behind the Law of Attraction and its connection with the *Bhagavad Gita*, it's time for you to learn the most important law which controls the Law of Attraction – like attracts like.

'Like attracts like' means energy with the same frequency will attract each other.

Scientists discovered that even though there is a single energy in the universe, energy always vibrates at different frequencies. When these frequencies match, they attract each other. Scientists made magical inventions based on this Law of Attraction. Here are three important inventions of our age which would have not been possible without the discovery of like attracts like.

Telephone – If you dial in the frequency of your friend's number, it will connect to the same frequency.

Television – When you switch to a particular channel, the TV will attract the same channel frequency.

Radio – If you tune into a radio frequency of 94.3 MHz then it will attract 94.3 MHz frequency perfectly, nothing else.

Since we are made of energy, whatever frequency we vibrate at, we will attract the same energy frequency.

Two Types of Frequencies:

There are two types of frequencies around us all the time – positive and negative frequency.

> **What you think you become, what you feel you attract, what you imagine you create.**
>
> –Buddha

If you are vibrating at a positive frequency you will attract more positive energy but if you vibrate at a negative frequency, you will also attract negative energy to yourself.

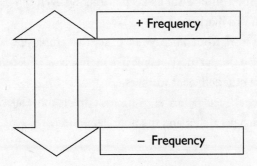

We use the Law of Attraction unconsciously as we always vibrate at a certain frequency (positive or negative) and constantly attract the same energy to ourselves in the form of people and situations. Here are multiple examples of people and situations with the same frequency attracting each other:

- In school you may have observed how the naughty children sit together while the studious team up because people with like energy will always attract each other.
- People who speak the same language will always try and stay together in keeping with the 'community' feeling. Our community is nothing but a group of like-minded individuals attracting each other.
- Sometimes when we think of a friend and he calls us, it is because both were probably thinking about each other at the same time and thus attracted each other at the same frequency.
- When we fear something, we desperately wish that it doesn't happen to us; yet, it happens and this is because the more we are scared the more we attract that frequency towards us.
- You must have observed that many businesses have their own market areas. For example, there are electronic market, wholesale market, vegetables market, hardware market, computer market, cloth market, jewellery market and many more. These markets are not always consciously planned, but because they have the same frequency, similar shops keep attracting each other and it slowly becomes a market.
- If you work from office, you will see that employees who complain and crib, attract more people like themselves, while efficient people attract other efficient workers.
- Failure attracts failure and success attracts more success.
- The rich get richer and the poor get poorer.

- Angry people attract more angry situations.
- Happy people attract opportunities to be happy.
- Sad people attract more sad people to talk to and more situations that make them feel sad.
- I see that people who have happy and healthy relationships attract more such friends whereas people who constantly have bad relationships are also surrounded by similar friends.
- This book is also matter which is made of energy; after you read this book, you will attract more books on the topic of the Law of Attraction. Or you might have attracted this book because you have been thinking or talking about this topic or might have bought a book with similar energy frequency.
- Honest people will attract more honest people and situations where honesty works; liars will attract more people who are liars and situations where they find it necessary to lie.

I can go on and on to give you examples as there is unlimited proof around you to demonstrate that like attracts like. All of life works as per this simple law of attraction – like attracts like.

Now given a choice, what would you like to attract – positive people and situations or negative people and situations?

You may think of this as a silly question. After all, everyone wants to attract positive people and situations. While this is true, the problem is that most people don't know how to control their own energy frequency.

Many times people vibrate at a negative frequency and attract negative people and situations; they then tag the situation as bad luck. But the fact is that our attractions depend on our own frequency.

What if you could learn how to control your frequency? You would be able to attract more positive energy, lots of good luck, lots of positive people and situations and avoid negative energy and thus also avoid what is called 'bad luck'.

Here is a story of a CEO who attracted a business excellence award using the Law of Attraction. (I have not revealed his name for confidential reasons.)

This CEO is a very famous personality who had been working with a multinational organization for about two years and six months. He was nominated for the business excellence award.

Even though he was nominated, his chances of getting the award were slim because the award required him to be a CEO for at least three years.

He was a worthy candidate and had worked hard for the award but luck too had to support him. This is where I used the visualization and recording techniques with him to help him attract this award (You will learn about these techniques in Chapter 7).

Using the Law of Attraction, he succeeded in winning the award by tuning himself to the exact frequency of his goal.

In the next chapter, you too shall learn how to control your frequency so you can control what you attract in your life. But before that do the following exercise which will prepare you for it.

Exercise:

Where in your life do you see the proof of the Law of Attraction working negatively and positively both?

While writing the answer, check what you are attracting in different areas of your life, like:

- Friends
- Income levels
- Repetitive problems
- Relationships
- Achievements

- Failures and success
- Health

Write down the answer to this question before you move on to the next topic.

When you do this exercise you will realize that whatever you attract in your life is a result of your own frequency.

It is your own energy frequency which attracts negative or positive people and situations in your life.

At this point, I usually ask an important question in my Law of Attraction workshops: Now that you have learnt how like attracts like, what is your biggest learning?

Please take the time to write down your learning before you continue to read.

_____

_____

_____

_____

Let me share my own answer with you:

My biggest learning is that I am responsible for everything in my life.

Until I learnt about the Law of Attraction, the statement that I am responsible for my life was just a statement which I thought was morally right. Now I have the scientific basis to understand how exactly I am responsible for my life. It is my own frequency that attracts all that happens in my life.

In the next chapter you will learn the difference between what you attract and what you are destined for. You will gain much more from the next chapter after you complete the above exercise and write down your learning from the principle of 'like attracts like'.

At this point a common question that people ask me is…

Like Attracts Like or Opposites Attract?

This question has confused many practitioners of the Law of Attraction, including me in the initial stages. Even in my workshops people ask me if like attracts like, how is it that opposites attract? Here is the answer to this question.

In school we learnt that the same sides of a magnet repel while opposite sides attract. We also learnt that energy with the same frequency will always attract each other, like in the case of radio frequency.

This might seem like a contradiction but actually they complement each other. Let me explain how.

Like attracts like and opposites attract – what this means is energy compatibility. Energy will always attract its compatible energy to itself.

Here are some examples to understand this:

Lock and key, male and female, buyer and seller, opportunities and challenges – these may seem to be opposites, but they function at par because of their energetic compatibility.

They are compatible because they are incomplete without each other. So actually they are two sides of the same energy attracting each other to become whole again.

The same is true for 'like attracts like', which means that compatible energy will always attract each other.

So if you want to attract success, you must learn to vibrate at its compatible energy frequency; if you want to attract money you must learn to attract its compatible energy frequency and if you want to attract happiness you must learn to vibrate at its compatible energy frequency.

The following chapter reveals how you can use the Law of Attraction to create compatible energy frequency to attract whatever you want in your life.

Summary of Like Attracts Like

- The Law of Attraction is controlled by the law 'like attracts like'.
- 'Like attracts like' means energy with the same frequency attract each other.
- Scientifically, 'like attracts like' has been proven with inventions like the telephone, television and radio.
- Since we are made of energy, we will attract the same energy frequency at which we vibrate.
- There are two types of frequencies: positive or high energy frequency and negative or low energy frequency.
- Positive attracts positive and negative attracts negative frequency.
- It is your own frequency which attracts negative or positive situations and people in your life.
- We are responsible for everything we attract in our life.
- What is really meant by 'like attracts like' and 'opposites attract' is energetic compatibility, which means that compatible energy will always attract each other.

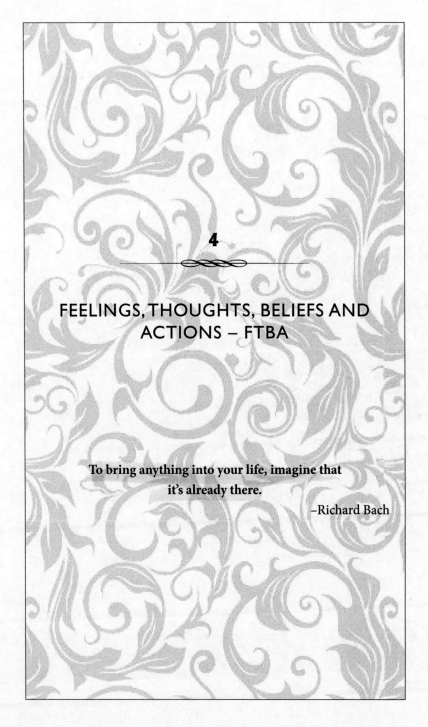

4

$\approx\!\!\approx\!\!\approx$

FEELINGS, THOUGHTS, BELIEFS AND ACTIONS – FTBA

To bring anything into your life, imagine that
it's already there.

–Richard Bach

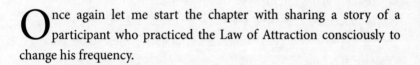

Once again let me start the chapter with sharing a story of a participant who practiced the Law of Attraction consciously to change his frequency.

Hello Mitesh,

I have lots to share with you, but for now I will share only some of my best experiences.

I always wanted to work abroad and wanted an onsite opportunity from my company at least once before my marriage.

I work in a product-based company where it is very difficult to get onsite opportunity unless we have a minimum of two and a half years of experience.

As per this policy, I was not eligible and thus I was quite disappointed because I had very little time before I tied the knot. I really wanted to work in a foreign country and enjoy my bachelor life.

That's when my friend Lavesh introduced me to your Law of Attraction workshop.

Attending this workshop was a great experience. I learnt a lot of new and exciting things about myself, about life, and the powers that are hidden within me.

I started using the Law of Attraction and started manifesting an onsite opportunity.

I started thinking positively and created massive positive energy around me; I started believing that I already had an on-site opportunity.

With practice my feelings became stronger. In just three months there came an opportunity in my company and I knew that I would be the one chosen to travel.

Finally the day came and on 14th September 2014, I got the opportunity to go to Japan for three months. I returned on 14th December 2014, after almost three months.

In Japan too I followed the same techniques. I did very well at my workplace and got another opportunity for more than three months this time.

So I will be travelling again on 4th January 2015. I started believing in myself and started demonstrating my best performance at work.

I can't say how happy and confident I feel after this miraculous experience. Thanks a lot Mitesh, for such a wonderful workshop and for the Law of Attraction techniques you taught me.

I would like to thank my roommate and best friend Lavesh Agrawal for introducing me to this amazing power of Law of Attraction and helping me realize my true potential.

Thanks and Regards,

Manoj Chavan

In the previous chapter we have learnt that like attracts like but now let's see how we can use this understanding to attract what we want in our life.

All our desires, all our goals are made of matter which is made of energy and has a specific frequency. For example, our desires – relationships, cars, houses, money – all these are made of energy and have their specific energy frequencies.

If you learn to vibrate at the exact frequency of your goals then it is logical that you will attract them because like attracts like.

So if we want a car, we must vibrate at the exact frequency of the car to attract it.

If we want a house, we must vibrate at the exact frequency of the house to attract it.

If we want a relationship, we must vibrate at the exact frequency of the relationship to attract it.

Whatever we want, the only way to attract it is to vibrate at its exact frequency. *We must learn to control our frequency so that we can control what we attract.*

In order to control the frequency at which we vibrate, we must first understand what our frequency is made of.

What is Our Frequency Made of?

Our Energy frequency is made of four elements, the FTBAs:

- Feelings
- Thoughts
- Beliefs
- Actions

Consider your mind, heart and body is like a radio which is constantly transmitting a certain energy frequency. By now you know that the energy you transmit is the energy you attract, whether positive or negative.

The feelings, thoughts and beliefs in your heart are energy vibrating at a certain frequency. The actions you take also have a certain frequency.

Thus, through your feelings, thoughts, beliefs and actions, you always transmit certain energy frequency in the universe which in turn attracts its matching frequency.

So if you want to attract your goals, you must learn to tune your frequency (your FTBAs) at the exact matching frequency of your goals.

If the frequency of your goals is 91.3 MHz, you must learn to tune your frequency (your FTBAs) exactly to 91.3 MHz.

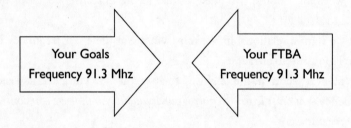

This is just like getting the right frequency on your radio. If your tuning is off by even a single digit, it will not attract the radio channel of your desire. The frequency has to be perfect.

How do we know the exact frequency of our goals?

Unlike a radio channel, there is no way to measure the frequency of your goals in Mhz. So then how do we tune our frequency when we don't know the exact frequency of our goals?

The way to vibrate at the exact frequency of your goals
is to feel, think, believe and act (FTBA) as if
you already have it.

This is the magic that makes the Law of Attraction work. When you live your life as if you already have your goals, you are tuned into its exact matching frequency.

- If you want a car then feel, think, believe and act as if you already have a car.
- If you want a house then tune your FTBAs as if you already have a house.
- If you want a relationship then tune your FTBAs as if you already have a relationship.
- Whatever you want, just feel, think, believe and act as if you already have it.

> **Therefore I say to you, all things for which you pray and ask, believe that you have received them, and they will be granted to you.**
> – Mark 11:24, King James Bible

The most successful people in the world knew this secret and thus they mastered the art of tuning their frequency to their goals. Here are some examples:

This is a letter that Bruce Lee wrote to himself…

I, Bruce Lee, will be the first highest paid oriental super star in the United States. In return, I will give the most exciting performance and render the best of quality in the capacity of an actor. Starting 1970, I will achieve world fame and from then onwards till the end of 1980, I will have in my possession $10,000,000. I will live the way I please and achieve inner harmony and happiness.

Bruce Lee
January 1969

Jim Carrey, the Hollywood superstar, wrote a check to himself for
$10 million for acting services, dated Thanksgiving Day, 1995.
     He actually made $10 million for the movie Dumb & Dumber
just before Thanksgiving Day in 1995.

There are many examples of successful people who knew that their success was inevitable. They know that it is important to feel, think, believe and act as if they are already successful in what they want.

This is not what most people do. Most people have negative feelings like:

- Fear
- Jealousy
- Helplessness
- Anxiousness and
- Impatience to achieve their goals

They think negative thoughts like:

- What if I don't get what I want.
- It's very difficult to get what I want.
- Life is not fair.
- It will take too much time, etc.

With such feelings, thoughts and beliefs people have negative actions which take them in the opposite direction from their goals.

Remember the personal genie within you? Your genie is
your FTBA which is like a magnet attracting more of its 'like
frequency' to you in the form of people and situations.

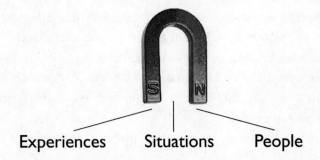

Experiences   Situations   People

If you feel, think, believe and act negatively, *negative frequency* people and situations will get attracted to you like a magnet. For example, if you FTBA as if you always meet people who cheat you, you will attract people who *will* cheat you.

If you feel, think, believe and act positive, *positive frequency* people and situations will get attracted to you like a magnet. For example, if you FTBA as if you always meet good people, you *will* attract good people in your life.

A lot of my Law of Attraction participants ask me:

From where do we attract such situations and people?

Well, positive and negative frequencies are always around you, it's you who tunes into them and attracts them.

When you tune in a radio, the matching frequency is always around you, it's just that your radio tunes into it. That's why it's called tuning into the right frequency. Similarly, negative and positive people are always around, you just tune into them.

Haven't you seen some people experiencing good luck while others experience bad luck within the same environment or office? How does that happen?

It's because one person unconsciously tunes into the negative frequency and thus attracts all the bad luck despite the hard work they do. Another person may be tuned into positive frequency and thus attracts all the good luck despite being ordinary at their work.

Do you now see how we may be unconsciously using the Law of Attraction against ourselves! Even at an unconscious level whatever we feel, think, believe and act, we attract the same.

Thus we are responsible for the quality of life that we attract, whether it is positive or negative. Nothing can come to us unless we are vibrating at its matching frequency!

So once again, how do we tune into the exact frequency of our goals?

The way to tune into the exact frequency of our goals is to feel, think, believe and act as if you already have it.

As long as we are alive, we generate positive or negative frequency with our FTBAs all the time.

Have you ever been secretly angry with a friend? Have you noticed that after a few days you see a change in his behaviour towards you as if he knows that you are having negative thoughts about him? If you have, ask yourself: how did your friend feel something is wrong even though you did not say anything?

That's because when you started vibrating at a negative energy frequency towards him, you transmitted that frequency to him. And since all of us are made of the same energy, it is easy for us to sense each other's frequencies, especially if we are close friends.

Similarly, if you think negatively about your boss, you will transmit negative energy to him and he will respond with similar energy frequency through his FTBAs.

If you feel low, bored or frustrated for some reason, be assured that it will attract its matching frequency to you in the form of people and situations which we generalize as 'bad luck'.

If you feel happy, peaceful and confident, you will transmit this positive energy in your environment and attract people and situations that have the same positive energy. This is how we unconsciously attract positive things in life which we then call 'good luck'.

Here is an example of Madhusudhan; he approached me for coaching when he was unable to get a job.

Madhu came to me because he had left his job three months ago and since then he had given more than 10 interviews, but he was unable to get employment anywhere.

During our coaching, I asked him how he felt, thought, believed and acted at the time he left his previous job.

This was his answer:

Feelings	Stressed, overwhelmed, unhappy, frustrated, helpless, and angry. He hated his job.
Thoughts	There is too much politics here. Boss is very dominating. Colleagues are not good people. Too much work pressure. There is no growth here.
Beliefs	This is my bad luck. Not possible to be happy in such a company. I always get people who take advantage of me. It's better not to have a job than work for a company like this.
Actions	Going to the office unwillingly, working without passion, arguing with colleagues, cribbing about the organization, looking for another job. Finally, he resigned without having a job in hand.

Looking at this table, Madhusudhan realized why he was facing problems in his previous job. With such a negative FTBA frequency it was natural to attract negative people and situations which made him leave his job.

Then I asked him about his FTBA since the last three months.

Feelings	Stressed, overwhelmed, unhappy, frustrated, helpless, angry and worried.
Thoughts	It is difficult to get a job because the market is down. I am not sure what line of job I should take. What if I get a job with the same problems? What will happen if I don't get a job?
Beliefs	This is my bad luck. It is not possible to be happy without a job. Life is not fair to me.
Actions	Getting up late in the morning since there is no office, wasting time with friends, spending a lot of time alone at home feeling lonely and unlucky, giving interviews but without the confidence required.

I helped Madhusudhan discover that based on his current FTBAs it was not possible for him to attract a job. You cannot attract positive frequency while being tuned into a negative frequency.

He was tuned into not having a job. No wonder he did not clear any of his interviews. It was a case of wrong frequency, not bad luck. Unconsciously he was using his FTBAs to attract more and more negativity in his life.

Madhusudhan now understood why he wasn't getting a job, but his question was how to tune into the right frequency to attract a job.

The answer is the same as earlier. Feel, think, believe and act as if you already have the job.

I asked Madhusudhan how he would feel, think, believe and act as if he had already cleared an interview for his dream job that he was supposed to join in a week.

This was his answer:

Feelings	Happy, excited, grateful, relieved, relaxed, satisfied and looking forward to joining his new office next week.
Thoughts	Finally I have got a job. Thank God! I was really lucky to get a job in such a big company, I am sure I will find good people, good work and a great boss in this new company. I will do my work with passion this time.
Beliefs	Life is good. I will have a great career path in this company. It's a great new beginning for me. I deserved this opportunity.
Actions	Get up early every day so I get used to getting up early by my joining date. I will go shopping for some new shirts for the first day of my job. I will celebrate with my friends and family. I will start reading my work related books to upgrade myself.

This was the required FTBA frequency.

I helped him to use a visualization technique to imagine all the above, as if he already has his dream job with the salary that he had in mind. (You will learn this technique in Chapter 7.)

After using the visualization technique, he felt wonderful and realized the importance of feeling positive in order to attract a job. He then practiced this new FTBA frequency for a week and got his dream job in just a week after that.

This is the magic of the Law of Attraction. Experience this magic for yourself by doing the following exercise: whenever something goes wrong in your life and you want to know how you attracted it and how to change your attraction, just do the following exercise to get all your answers.

Exercise: Taking Control of Your FTBA Frequency

Now take any area of your life and recognize your negative FTBAs, your
negative frequency.

Feelings

Thoughts

Beliefs

Actions

Now take the same area of your life and create your positive FTBAs,
your positive frequency.

Feelings

Thoughts

Beliefs

Actions

Now stop the negative feelings, thoughts, beliefs and actions and start the positive FTBAs as per the above table to attract positive results.

What you attract is in your hands now, all you need to do is use the above exercise to change and tune your frequency to your desired goals.

The next chapter will now explain the difference between your destiny and your attractions.

Summary of FTBA

- Whatever we want, the only way to attract it is to vibrate at its exact frequency.
- We must learn to control our frequency so we can control what we attract.
- Our frequency is made of our feelings, thoughts, beliefs and actions (FTBAs).
- If you want to attract your goals then you must learn to tune your frequency (your FTBAs) at the exact matching frequency of your goals.
- The way to vibrate at the exact frequency of your goals is to feel, think, believe and act as if you already have it.
- Most people have negative FTBAs which take them away from their goals.
- Positive and negative frequencies are always around you, it's you who tunes into them and attracts them.
- In order to change the frequency, first recognize your negative attractions and their frequency.
- Create positive attractions by creating positive frequency.

5

CONTROLLING THE CYCLE OF ATTRACTION

*Once you make a decision, the universe conspires
to make it happen.*

–Ralph Waldo Emerson

With years of research I discovered what I call the Cycle of Attraction.

The cycle of attraction answers two very important questions:

1. How do we know the difference between what we are destined for and what we attract in our life?
2. Is it not natural to feel negative when we experience negative situations?

To get the answers to these questions let's learn how the cycle of attraction works. To start with, this is what the cycle of attraction looks like:

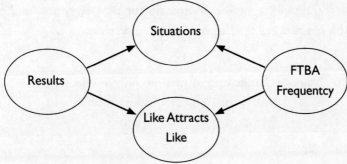

When a situation occurs, we respond to it with our feelings, thoughts, beliefs and actions (FTBA Frequency) which the Law of Attraction uses to attract certain results, which in turn creates more situations of the same frequency for us.

For example, when people experience a breakup, they respond to it by feeling sad, angry, helpless, or inferior; they may also feel that they don't deserve love. They may question their fate and the breakup. As a result, they stay aloof, away from relationships, in a stressful condition for a long time.

With such negative FTBA, people attract negative results which in turn attract more negative situations in every area of their life. This is what I call the *Negative Cycle of Attraction*.

However, there are people who respond to the same situation with a much more positive FTBA. They too feel low but for some time and quickly take control of their emotions, feel hopeful for a better relationship while thinking and focusing on what they have rather than what they don't have. They believe and have faith that sometimes breakups are natural and that they will soon attract the love of their life. In fact, they believe that the breakup happened to make them a better human being.

With such positive FTBAs they act positively, they forgive the person who broke up with them, they focus on a much better future and keep their heart open for love.

With this kind of positive FTBA frequency, they attract positive results and thus attract more positive situations in every area of their life. This is what I call the *Positive Cycle of Attraction*.

**You can change your attractions only by changing
your FTBA frequency!**

If you become aware of your cycle of attraction, you can change your attractions, results and situations simply by changing your FTBA frequency.

Most people are slaves to their feelings, thoughts, beliefs and habitual actions. This book will show you how to take control and become a master of your FTBAs so that you can deliberately change your frequency and take control of your attractions.

Here is a story of a businessman who stopped the negative cycle of attractions and started a positive cycle of attractions in his business.

Pramod was running a successful business of teaching physics to thousands of students in partnership with a friend.

He did not expect his friend to betray him so he did not get his partnership legally registered. As it happened, his partner cheated him and took away the business, leaving him with nothing.

When Pramod came to me, he was devastated and had absolutely no money left in his account; he didn't know how to re-establish himself.

When I explained the Law of Attraction to him he was amazed to know how his own subject, physics, had the solution to all his problems.

He was not sure whether his friend had cheated him because he had attracted the action or whether it was his bad luck. However, he realised that he could break this negative cycle of attraction and start a positive cycle of attraction.

He used the gratitude technique (explained in Chapter 8) and told me that he would call me back in a few days once he had attracted what he wanted.

In just three days he called me to tell me that he had got a financier who was willing to fund him; he had already got an office and even convinced a group of his previous students to join his tuitions.

In fact, when he called he said he was calling from his new office. He sounded very happy and excited but most importantly, he sounded grateful to the universe for giving him what he wanted.

Such miracles are possible when you practice the Law of Attraction techniques.

Here again is the question with which we started this chapter.

How do we know the difference between what we are destined for and what we attract in our life?

From years of personal experience in using the Law of Attraction, my opinion is that about 80 per cent of our life situations are attractions that we can control and 20 per cent is our destiny which is not in our control.

Perhaps our destiny or destination is fixed, but how we experience the journey of reaching our destination is completely in our hands.

Helen Keller was probably destined to be deaf and blind. How she experienced her life journey in this condition or despite it was completely in her hands. She chose to take control of how she felt, what she thought, what she believed and thus she took control of her actions which in turn created extraordinary results and situations in her life.

So while the tough news is that 20 per cent of your life is not in your hands, the good news is that 80 per cent is, if you learn to control your FTBAs.

Now the tricky part is that no one really knows exactly which situation comes in the 20 per cent area of your destiny or in the 80 per cent area which you attracted.

For example, if you had an accident while driving, there are 80 per cent chances that unconsciously you may have attracted that accident. It is also possible that no matter how positive you are, there is always that 20 per cent possibility of your going through an accident if you were destined for it.

Nobody can tell with absolute guarantee whether this accident was your attraction or your destiny.

Consider the case of a child born without hands and legs. This is probably his destiny since he was born like this. Some people may argue that the child is born with a disability because of his past karma. This may be true but there is really no way of proving whether the child attracted this situation or was destined for it.

So what do we do then? How do we know which part of our life is our destiny and which our own attraction?

While there is no definite answer to this question, my opinion is that it is best to consider that 100 per cent of our life is our attraction so there is no confusion.

Just focus on controlling your feelings, thoughts, beliefs and actions because in the cycle of attraction, that's the only area which is in our complete control.

While we may be destined for some problems, challenges, accidents, misfortunes or bad luck in our life, how we respond to that through our FTBAs is definitely 100 per cent in our control. Nobody can take that choice away from us.

Here is the second question with which we started this chapter.

Is it not natural to feel negative when we experience negative situations?

No, it is not always natural to feel negative when we experience negative situations. It is natural for plants to be green, it is natural for the sun to rise in the morning, it is natural to live and die. The word natural means nature controls it, not we. When someone talks to you badly it is not natural for you to feel bad. By changing your thinking you can change the way you feel, which means it is in your control. The trick is to not react habitually to negative situations in a negative manner. No matter how many disadvantages and negative situations you experience, you can always choose to control your FTBAs and influence your attractions. Here are some examples that illustrate this.

Ordinary people let their situations define their FTBAs; extraordinary people use their FTBAs to define their situations.

People like Oprah Winfrey, Amitabh Bachchan, Narayan Murthy, Bill Gates, Steve Jobs and Milkha Singh are legends who started their career with many disadvantages and through negative situations. By controlling their FTBAs, they controlled their life attractions.

I personally started with a lot of disadvantages when I started my career as a corporate leadership trainer. People said I didn't have the qualification, the potential, the credibility, the knowledge, or what it takes to be a good leadership trainer.

Yes, I had all these disadvantages, but then I thought that there was one common thing about great trainers, actors, authors, businessmen, teachers, musicians and sports legends: they were all nothing when they started.

If they could start with nothing, so could I. With such thoughts, I continued working towards my goals and thus I attracted luck, opportunities, clients, mentors and experiences that helped me to become the person I am today and live the beautiful life that I have. I created a Positive Cycle of Attraction.

The crux of the matter is that if you take control of your FTBAs, you can take control of your life. As for the remaining 20 per cent, only its occurrence is beyond your control, not its impact on your life, not how you decide to face it.

When I started writing my first book, I was told that it's almost impossible for a common man like me to establish myself as an author. People said I wouldn't be able to write well because I didn't have the skills of an author and even if I did manage to write a book, I wouldn't get a publisher to accept my book.

I was told stories of people who have been trying to publish their books for years despite being good writers. So what chance did I have?

I did not let any of this affect me or induce a Negative Cycle of Attraction. I decided to feel confident and emotionally strong. I thought and believed that I would be a bestselling author one day and started taking action to write my first bestselling book Awaken the Leader in You.

One of my favourite authors, Robin Sharma, had his books published by Jaico, so I used the Law of Attraction and asked my genie to help me write a great book and also get it accepted by Jaico Publishers.

I contacted Jaico on my own, without the help of any references or literary agents, and mailed my first manuscript to them. I got a response from them within a week, saying that they would like to meet me. In two weeks after my first meeting with Jaico, they sent me a contract to publish my book.

So while hundreds of writers may be struggling to get a book published by Jaico, how come I got a contract signed with them within two weeks of contacting them? And out of all the publishers, how did I get Jaico to start with!

I give all the credit to my genie, to the magic of the Law of Attraction. Now it is time for you to use your genie, your FTBA frequency to attract what you want.

From the next chapter you will learn how to change your frequency by using tried and tested techniques of Law of Attraction.

To start with make sure you do the FTBA exercise in the previous chapter to help you recognize and change your current frequency. For your convenience here is the exercise again...

Exercise: Taking Control of Your FTBA Frequency

Now take any area of your life and recognize your negative FTBAs, your negative frequency.

Feelings

_____

Thoughts

_____

Beliefs

_____

Actions

_____

Now take the same area of your life and create your positive FTBAs, your positive frequency.

Feelings

_____

Thoughts

_____

Beliefs

_____

Actions

_____

Summary of The Cycle of Attraction

- When a situation occurs, we respond to it with our feelings, thoughts, beliefs and actions (FTBA frequency) which the Law of Attraction uses to attract certain results, which in turn creates more situations of the same frequency for us.
- When we react negatively to a negative situation, we create a negative cycle of attraction.
- When we react positively to a negative situation, we create a positive cycle of attraction.
- You can change your attraction by changing your frequency, your FTBAs.
- Twenty per cent of your life is not in your hands, but the good news is that the rest of it is if you learn to control your FTBAs.
- No one knows for sure which situation is your destiny or your attraction.
- It is best to assume that 100 per cent of your life is your creation; it is not natural to feel negative about negative situations because we can control how we feel, think, believe and act in any situation.
- Ordinary people let their situations define their FTBAs while extraordinary people use their FTBAs to define their situations.

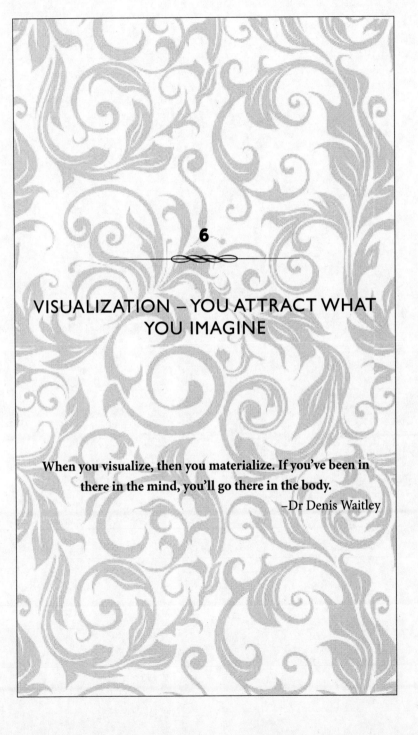

6

VISUALIZATION – YOU ATTRACT WHAT YOU IMAGINE

When you visualize, then you materialize. If you've been in
there in the mind, you'll go there in the body.
                                                    –Dr Denis Waitley

Remember that everything is made of matter which is made of energy that vibrates at a certain frequency.

So if you have a goal of attracting a car or a house or a relationship, it is also made of matter which is made of energy vibrating at a certain frequency.

In our case we use the FTBAs as a radio to tune into the exact frequency of our goals. If you feel, think, believe and act as if you already have what you want, only then you will attract it.

You can't attract what you want; you can only attract what you already have in your energy frequency.

One of the best techniques to tune into the frequency of your goals is the *Visualization Technique.*

In order to tune into the frequency of your goals, you must visualize that you have already achieved your goal. For example, you can visualize that you already have your dream car and house. By doing this, you are tuning into the exact frequency of your goals and thus attracting them towards you.

Now we can use this understanding and use visualization to create specific frequency vibrations and attract anything we want.

Here are the three simple steps to the Visualization Technique:

Step 1 – Be clear and specific – Be clear and specific about what you want. This is the first step to attract what you want because if you do not have the clarity of purpose, you will attract random frequencies. So make sure that you start with 100 per cent clarity regarding what you want to attract.

If it's a car that you want to attract, then be clear and specific about the model, colour, type and also the time by when you want to attract it. If it's a relationship, be clear and specific about what kind of person you want to attract in terms of looks, nature and the timeline for fulfilment. Whatever you want, it is necessary to visualize it with complete clarity.

Step 2 – Relax and visualize – Now close your eyes and relax by taking a few deep breaths. By doing this you drop your brain frequency between 7 MHz and 14 MHz which is the most effective frequency to attract other frequencies.

Once you relax, visualize that you have already achieved your goal in the present state of mind. When you visualize that you already have it, you are tuning into its frequency and starting to attract it towards you like a radio channel. Make sure that when you visualize it, you make it as real in your mind as possible with a lot of emotional energy.

For example, right now imagine you are on your dream holiday travelling in business class, staying in a 5-Star resort, sitting next to the swimming pool with an iced tea or a beer in your hands.

This is important during all techniques of Law of Attraction; you must think of your goals as if you have already achieved them. By imagining it happening in the present moment and feeling happy about it, your energy vibrates at its exact frequency so you can attract it.

Step 3 – Feel grateful and let go – At the end of the visualization, make sure that you feel a lot of gratitude for having it. Thank God and magnify the feeling of gratitude. Gratitude is one of the most powerful frequencies in the world. Whenever we achieve something we naturally feel grateful and end up saying 'Thank God!'

So we deliberately generate the 'thank you' frequency to perfectly tune into the frequency of already having your goals. Once you feel grateful, let go of the thought knowing that you already have it. During the day, don't have any thoughts, worries and doubts. Don't get restless about attracting it.

Remember that you are supposed to feel, think, believe and act as if you already have it. Then how can you get worried or have doubts or get restless? Do you get restless for what you already have? No you don't, because you already have it!

You must do the visualization technique three times in a day:

1. Every morning as soon as you wake up.
2. Every night just before you sleep.
3. Anytime you are in a negative state of mind.

How I Used the Visualization Technique

I personally use visualization every single day of my life, every morning and every night, and have reaped extraordinary benefits from this simple technique to attract many goals of my life. Here are a couple of examples for your reference:

Once I had a small accident and suffered a back injury which was diagnosed as slip disc and sciatica. After this accident, I experienced acute pain in my back and left leg 24 hours a day.

I started feeling bad for myself and did not realize that by feeling bad about myself, I was actually generating a stronger frequency of being ill rather than being cured. I went to many doctors, joined yoga, and did physiotherapy, acupuncture, acupressure and tried many other alternative treatments. Nothing helped. I started thinking and believing that there was no cure to my problem. After nine months of suffering from slip disc and sciatica, I decided to use the magic of Law of Attraction to cure myself.

I know it sounds insane to use the Law of Attraction for a health problem which can only be cured by medical science, but I had tried everything else and the Law of Attraction was my last resort.

So I started using the visualization technique every day and saw myself cured already, I felt grateful and I let go of it believing that it is already done. In the day time I started ignoring the pain, stopped cribbing about it and started acting as if I am completely cured.

In just a couple of days after that I was invited to a Law of Attraction workshop conducted by a monk called Nithyashanti. It cannot be a coincidence that after I created a frequency of being cured, I attracted a Law of Attraction workshop, I thought.

That day my situation was so bad that I couldn't even sit straight in a chair for more than 10 minutes so there was a special bed arranged for me on which I could lie down in order to attend the workshop.

In this workshop, whenever we practiced the visualization technique, I saw myself cured and living my life healthy and strong. That evening when I was going home, I suddenly remembered a friend called Ram who had met me a year ago. Ram had said that even he had sciatica but had it cured with a small surgery.

All this time I had not thought of this friend but now that I was tuned into the right frequency, of being cured, I remembered something that could help me.

I immediately called Ram and asked him about this surgery. He said it was a very small keyhole surgery called Laparoscopy, a 30-minute procedure; that and a couple of days of rest was all that I would require.

How had I missed out on this information for so long! He gave me his doctor's number. I called the doctor, Dr Pradhyuman Pairaiturkar, and took an appointment for the next morning.

He did some tests and got me admitted in the hospital; that night my surgery was done and immediately afterwards the doctor helped me raise my leg straight up by 90 degrees. After a long time, my back and legs felt normal. There was no pain.

All this happened in only a week after I started using the visualization technique.

When you use the visualization technique, you are consciously transmitting the exact frequency of what you want to attract in your life.

Like attracts like is a law that works every time, just like the law of gravity. So be assured and start using the visualization technique today.

This is the story of a participant from my Law of Attraction workshop. When she left the workshop, she was quite sceptical about how the Law of Attraction would help her achieve her goals. Since she was logically convinced with all the scientific facts I shared in the workshop, she decided to give it a shot.

A few weeks after that she sent me an email telling me how she used the visualization technique to attract a job in Australia. She said that she knew it was difficult to get a job in Australia but she had decided to curb her negative feelings and thoughts and use the visualization technique to create the frequency of already having the job.

In three weeks she got an interview call from Australia which she gave on a video conference call; she was selected in the very first round. In her email she mentioned that she would be leaving for

Australia a month later and thanked me for making her realize the
magic she had within her.

Most people take action to create results but their feelings, thoughts and beliefs are in conflict with their actions. Using the Law of Attraction techniques, when you align your feelings, thoughts and beliefs with your actions, you are guided by the universe and your subconscious mind to take the right action and thus create the right results.

Now it's your turn to use this magic in your life and send me your success story by email.

Attracting Problems Unconsciously

> **Remember, we are always responsible for what we attract**
> **in our life because we are the only ones generating**
> **our energy frequency.**

Now let's understand how we unknowingly use the Law of Attraction techniques against ourselves and attract problems and what we call 'bad luck' in our life.

When we want something, we unconsciously start visualizing the problems we may face in achieving that goal, we get worried, we doubt whether we will achieve it and we get restless about when we will get to the goal.

A classic example is when a guy wants to attract a girl with whom he is infatuated. In these situations, many men unconsciously visualize the girl getting angry and rejecting them if they approach her. They talk about how they are not good enough to impress her, they get jealous and worried when they see the girl talking to someone else.

With emotions of worry, jealousy, doubt, restlessness, lack of confidence and desperation, they visualize the girl not being interested, not getting her attention and not being able to impress her. This kind of negative visualization creates negative actions from them which attract negative energy from the girl leading to her reacting negatively and rejecting the guy.

With such negative results they get more negative feelings, thoughts and beliefs and they take more negative actions which further attracts problems for them in their relationships. This creates a negative cycle of attraction for them in their relationships.

On the other hand, there are those who have unconsciously created positive FTBAs about approaching a girl. They are confident, they think and believe that they are attractive enough for a girl to respond to them positively and thus they act very confidently and positively. These guys naturally have a better chance of getting a positive response from girls most of the times.

When a girl rejects them, they take it lightly; they believe that it is alright to face some rejections in life till they meet the right person. So they continue to act with confidence while approaching other girls. With such positive FTBAs they create a positive cycle of attraction and thus eventually attract positive results in relationships.

Your feelings, thoughts, beliefs and actions create a frequency and attract more of the same towards you. Unfortunately, most people are unaware of this science and thus unconsciously create many negative frequencies through negative FTBAs.

Take the example of a workplace where a person's goal is to get a promotion. Most people again unconsciously visualize having an argument with their boss during their appraisals. They even talk to their friends about how difficult it is to get a promotion and get worried that the boss will not give them the promotion even if they have worked hard for it.

As a result of these negative FTBAs, they tune into a negative energy frequency of not getting the promotion which in turn attracts negative frequencies in the form of problems that finally deprives them of what they seek.

They then call this their bad luck, blame it on the boss, on the market situation, and other external factors.

If you truly want to be a master of your attractions, you must be aware of what you visualize. What you visualize (consciously or unconsciously) creates your frequency, your feelings, thoughts, beliefs and actions.

Now some participants tell me that they find it difficult to visualize. If you feel the same, don't worry.

In the next chapter, I share with you another powerful technique to apply the Law of Attraction. In fact this technique is probably the easiest, simplest and yet the most powerful techniques to apply the Law of Attraction.

Summary of Visualization

- If you learn to tune into the exact frequency of your goal, you can attract it towards you.
- Because you don't attract what you want, you attract what you already have in your energy frequency.
- One of the best techniques to tune into the frequency of your goals is the visualization technique.
- The visualization technique requires you to imagine and visualize that you have already achieved your goals.
- By doing this you tune into the exact frequency of your goals and thus attract it towards you.
- The three simple steps of the visualization technique:

    ▶ Be clear and specific
    ▶ Relax and visualize
    ▶ Be grateful and let go

- You must do the visualization technique three times in a day:

  ▶ Every morning
  ▶ Every night
  ▶ Anytime you are in a negative state of mind

- Even though we unknowingly feel, think, believe and act in a particular way, we always vibrate at a certain frequency, attract similar energy towards us.
- Thus we are always responsible for what we attract in our life.

7

FEELINGS – YOUR ENERGY IN MOTION

It doesn't matter what you want, you will attract what you feel.

Your feelings are the most potent form of energy and they are always in motion, working at a very high speed to attract their matching frequency.

As we discussed in Chapter 4, there are two types of frequencies: positive and negative. These frequencies are controlled by your feelings which are also positive and negative.

Here is a list of some positive and negative feelings for your reference:

Positive Feelings	Negative Feelings
Happiness	Sorrow
Love	Hatred
Hopefulness	Pessimism
Clarity	Confusion
Calmness	Irritation
Patience	Impatience
Liveliness	Boredom
Peace	Discord

| Strength | Weakness |
| Courage | Fear |

Until now you have only seen them as positive or negative feelings. Henceforth, I would like you to see them as energy vibrating at a positive or negative frequency.

Every day, every minute you feel something, thus you transmit energy of a certain frequency in the universe to attract its matching frequency.

For example, if you feel poor because of lack of money, you will attract more frequency of the same energy. This means that you will attract situations where you won't make enough money or you will lose money in some way. Most people call this bad luck but you are unconsciously using the Law of Attraction against yourself.

If you feel happy and grateful even during a financial crisis, you will attract more happy frequency energy. This means you will meet the right people, get the right opportunities and thus experience more happiness in your life. Most people call this good luck; actually you unconsciously use the Law of Attraction in your favour.

Here is an important question. Do you control your feelings or do your feelings control you?

If you are like most people, I am sure your feelings control you and thus control your attractions. To take control of your life attractions you must take control of how you feel.

Don't let situations and people impact your feelings; let your feelings impact them.

Here are some simple techniques to take control of your feelings. These techniques will not only help you control your feelings but also help you to control your thoughts, beliefs and actions. Feelings lead to thoughts, thoughts lead to beliefs and your beliefs lead to actions. So every technique I offer in this book will impact all your FTBAs at the same time because they are inter-connected.

However, for ease of understanding, I have categorized techniques for feelings, thoughts, beliefs and actions in different chapters. Here is the most powerful technique to take control of the frequency of your feelings.

Gratitude Technique – A Shortcut to Positive Attractions

A friend of mine (let's call him Jack) is a computer engineer and a genius at his work. He draws a fat salary from a multinational organization and has a great family that loves and supports him in every aspect of his life.

There was just one thing missing in his life. Happiness! If he had it all, why was he not happy? Are you bewildered?

He was not happy because he always complained about his life not being good enough. He never realized how lucky he was to have all that he did. Jack had a short temper and had very low tolerance for mistakes from anybody. Thus he was mostly annoyed at how people worked at office as well as at home.

He could not tolerate imperfections that people had. As a result of this attitude he was constantly vibrating at a frequency of cribs and complaints about everything and everybody in his life.

Since he always vibrated at a negative frequency, he started attracting negative energy from all directions. At one point his relationships in the office became so bad that he was fired from work without any explanation. Even in his personal life, the most important person who loved him also left him and slowly he saw his perfect life crumbling like a pack of cards.

He was in shock and did not realize why suddenly everything was going wrong in his life. In just a few days he had lost his job and his relationships; his family didn't believe in him anymore and nothing felt good.

For a long time he remained sad, angry and depressed, not realizing that he was increasing the negative attractions in his life.

One day his elder sister, who was a veteran practitioner of the Law of Attraction, helped him understand that he was responsible for all that was happening in his life. He was unconsciously using his genie against himself and attracting all the bad luck that he was experiencing.

She introduced him to the gratitude technique to stop attracting negative frequency and start attracting positive frequency.

What is the meaning of gratitude?
Gratitude simply means being grateful or thankful for what you have.

Being grateful is a feeling we experience whenever we get something good. For example:

- When you achieve your business goals you say 'Thank God'.
- When your problems are solved you say 'Thank God'.
- When you get a pleasant surprise gift you say 'Thank God'.
- When you realize how good your life is you say 'Thank God'.
- Every time you achieve something or something good happens in life you say 'Thank God' and feel grateful in your heart.

Thus the feeling of being grateful is a short cut to all positive attractions in your life. Think about it logically. When you vibrate at a frequency of being grateful, it means you already have what you want and start vibrating at the frequency of your desires.

As a result, magically you start attracting situations and people who will help you to achieve what you want. Your actions will be motivated in the right direction and even your subconscious mind will help you by keeping you motivated and positive. Beautiful, magical and surprising coincidences will help you to get what you want.

What ordinary people call coincidence, we call attraction.

It is said that Einstein also practiced gratitude by chanting, "Thank you for everything" during his regular walks.

All holy books such as the *Bhagavad Gita, Bible* and *Koran* teach us to be happy with what we have. What this really means is that we should vibrate at a frequency of gratitude rather than of complaints.

Focus on what you have rather than on what you don't have.

In the *Bhagavad Gita*, Lord Krishna explains to Arjuna, "*Karm kar, fal ki chinta mat kar*". Focus on your work, stop worrying about the results. Worrying about results will make you vibrate at a negative frequency and take you away from your goals.

Let us return to Jack's story. When he learnt about the Law of Attraction and the gratitude technique, suddenly everything became clear to him. He called his sister and told her that he had finally realized why he had lost his relationships and financial security.

Because he never had enough gratitude for them, he used to crib and complain about the imperfections in them. He realized how his complaints had turned into negative energy which he had attracted in the form of bad luck in his job and relationships.

Once Jack realized this, he started using the gratitude technique to feel grateful for all that he had and also for what he wanted, as if he already had it.

He started repeating to himself, "I am grateful for great relationships in my life, I am grateful for a successful career, I am grateful for everything that I have in my life right now, Thank you God for everything that I have in my life right now."

Jack repeated such gratitude statements to himself many times during the day and made a conscious effort to feel grateful instead of feeling sad, unhappy or any other negative emotional frequency.

By consciously creating the positive frequency of gratitude he tuned into positive attractions in just a few days.

As a result he got a new job in just a month after that. He started feeling more at peace than before because he was consciously making sure that he was in a state of gratitude rather than of complaints or unhappiness.

Even his relationships with his family and friends improved and life felt good again. All of this happened because Jack was vibrating at the gratitude frequency consciously.

Such is the power of gratitude!

Be thankful for what you have; you'll end up having more. If you concentrate on what you don't have, you will never, ever, have enough.

– Oprah Winfrey

Gratitude Exercise to Stop Negative Attractions and Start Positive Attractions:

- Write down all the areas of your life where you experience negative emotion.
- Stop feeling negative in these areas.
- Thank God for what you want in that area as if you already have it.
- Start focusing on what you have and be grateful for it; stop focusing on what you don't have.

By using this gratitude exercise you can change your frequency and thus stop all the negative attractions to ensure positive attractions in your life.

Here are multiple examples of how you can practice gratitude in your day to day life:

1. **When you get stuck in traffic in the morning**, stop complaining and thank God for giving you a clear road and helping you reach office on time. Make sure you feel grateful because you will transmit the same frequency to attract more of it.

2. **When you reach office and you are worried** that your client may not be convinced enough to give you what you want, stop being worried and say 'Thank God' for the client being supportive and understanding enough to give you exactly what you wanted. Feel the gratitude and go for the meeting with this positive energy. I bet you will influence the energy of the client and attract positive frequency from him.

3. **When you are having lunch and the cafeteria has something you don't like**, eat it with gratitude instead of complaining. This may not change the food in the cafeteria but it will help create a positive cycle of attraction for the rest of the day. However, if you get into a complaining mode it will create a negative cycle of attraction for the entire day. So be careful and experience gratitude.

4. **When you are leaving office and your work is not complete,** don't start getting tense and worried. Consciously express gratitude for

all that you have already completed and also thank God for helping you complete everything on time the next day. When you leave home with such a feeling of gratitude and positivity, you are bound to influence your family with this positive energy and make them happy as well.

5. **When you reach home and your life partner says something negative,** instead of giving an equally negative reaction, simply express gratitude for all that your partner has already done perfectly to make your life beautiful; ignore the trivial mistakes. Do the same with your children and you will see that this attitude of gratitude will help you attract more love and support from them than ever before!

6. **When you have financial problems,** don't get into self-pity or victim mode at the seeming lack of money in your life. If you do, then in that negative frequency of lack you will attract more financial problems. Everyone has financial problems, even a billionaire does. If you focus on what you have and experience gratitude, then you will realize that your basic needs are always taken care of. So just thank God for your basic financial needs being met and also thank God for giving you unlimited abundance in life. Vibrate at this abundant energy and you are sure to attract abundance rather than financial problems.

7. **If you are unhealthy,** don't get into the emotion of feeling low, irritated and weak. Consciously practice gratitude for the good health that you have had in the past and also express gratitude for the healing you are getting to regain health and vitality.

While you need to use gratitude to change your negative frequency into positive frequency, it is also important to use gratitude to maintain the positive frequency and attractions in your life.

What I mean is that right now, you and I are blessed with many things that we have in our life. This is also a result of some positive frequency attracting positive things in our life. Now this frequency needs to be maintained.

But when we are ungrateful for the things that we have, when we take them for granted, our frequency turns negative and interrupts the flow of positive frequency.

Let's understand how we can use gratitude to maintain our positive frequency attractions.

Gratitude Exercise to Maintain Positive Attractions in Your Life

I was attending a workshop where I was carrying a take-away cup of my favourite Starbucks coffee. A lady in the workshop was attracted to the aroma of my coffee and said she too loved Starbucks coffee. She asked me if I could bring a cup for her as well when I returned to the workshop the next day. I agreed and went out of my way to remember and bring her that coffee. When I entered the workshop the next day, I located her and gave her the cup. She looked at me, gave me a bland smile and walked away with her cup. She did not say anything!

I was quite surprised as she did not have the courtesy to thank me for my efforts or gesture. She behaved as if I were duty-bound to bring her the coffee. Do you think I would ever get her a cup of coffee again?

Such ungratefulness stops our positive frequency attractions.

Imagine when the universe gives us so many things and we forget to be grateful, how does the universe feel about it? The universe also feels bad because no one likes ungrateful behaviour. As a result, the universe stops giving us what we are not grateful for.

Now, I am not just talking about the big things that happen in life like promotions, achievement of goals or marriage. I refer here to all the small things that happen every day and for which we forget to say 'Thank You'.

Here is a list of things that happen every day for which we need to express gratitude so that we can maintain these positive attractions in our life:

1. Thank you for being alive every morning.
2. Thank you for my lovely family members.
3. Thank you for the health I have.
4. Thank you for my house and all the resources in it.
5. Thank you for my job.
6. Thank you for my lovely vehicle.
7. Thank you for safe roads and a safe city to live in.
8. Thank you for my office.
9. Thank you for the success I have at work.
10. Thank you for the colleagues who are good to me.
11. Thank you for the clients who give me business.
12. Thank you for the coffee I get in breaks.
13. Thank you for my lunch.
14. Thank you for a good day at work.
15. Thank you for the time I get with my family.
16. Thank you for the lovely weather I experience in my city.
17. Thank you for the friends I have in my life.
18. Thank you for the love I have in my life.
19. Thank you for my Laptop.
20. Thank you for my smartphone which keeps me connected.

The list can go on and on. Be grateful for all the things you have in your life so that you maintain the positive attractions. If you don't express gratitude and take them for granted, most likely those positive attractions will be taken away.

Take every opportunity to thank people for the small things they do for you, thank life for what it gives you every day, thank your family for the small things they do for you, be grateful for everything you get – and you will keep attracting more to be grateful for.

Wouldn't you appreciate someone who is always grateful to you for even the small things you do for them? Wouldn't you want to do more for them? That's exactly how you need to work with the universal Law of Attraction. By being grateful you vibrate at a positive frequency to which the Law of Attraction responds by giving you more positive attractions.

Here are three gratitude practices that I personally follow and invite you to practice them too:

1. **Morning gratitude** – When you get up every morning, remember to thank God for at least 10 things that you already have – another day for being alive, for your family, for the work you have, for the good health you have, for the house you have, for the food you have – and then thank God in advance for a great successful day ahead. Most importantly, say thank you for achieving all your goals as if you already have them.

2. **Night gratitude** – Repeat gratitude for everything you have in life and for everything that happened in life today before you sleep and also remember to say thank God for achieving all your goals as if you already have them. It is important that you sleep in a state of gratitude, not worries. Remember that you don't attract what you want, you attract what you are feeling. So sleep with the feeling of gratitude that you already have everything you want.

3. **Frequency-changing gratitude** – Whenever you are surrounded by difficult situations or people use gratitude to change your frequency. Simply start focusing on all the things that you can be grateful for. Also be grateful for the ideal result you want in those situations. For example, you are in a client meeting and the client is not giving you what you want. Instead of feeling worried and angry about it, simply repeat in your mind, "Thank you for the client being co-operative and happy with my work, thank you for a successful meeting with this client". Saying such gratitude statements will help you change your frequency to positive attractions. As a result,

your client who is also connected with the same energy will feel the difference in your energy and will respond positively.

I have used it with all my clients and always reaped extraordinary results. Try it out! Another example where you can use gratitude to instantly change your frequency is when you are looking for parking or looking for a taxi; just say to yourself, "Thank you God, for the parking or for the taxi", and then see how quickly you attract it compared to complaining for not having it.

If you are having conflicts in a relationship just say to yourself repeatedly, "Thank you God, for a happy and loving relationship" and then see how magically the conflicts get resolved. With positive feelings of gratitude, you get positive thoughts, beliefs and positive actions which will lead to attracting positive results for you.

Even when you are confused about making a decision and you don't know what to do, just repeat to yourself: "Thank you God, for giving me clarity in my decisions, I am feeling so clear and decisive now." When you repeat this, your subconscious mind will attract clear ideas to help you take clear decisions.

4. **Practice the attitude of gratitude during the entire day** – Take every opportunity during the day to loudly express your gratitude to people and to the universe.

    When your colleague does something for you, remember to thank them; when you leave a restaurant, remember to thank the waiters who served you; when you are at home having dinner with your family say thank you to your spouse for cooking the good dinner you had; when your children bring you a glass of water remember to thank them too.

    When you reach office, remember to say, "Thank you God, for a great day at work" before you even start the day; when you achieve small success during the day at work remember to say thank you to the universe.

    What I am saying is that we must express gratitude at every

opportunity so that we maintain the positive frequency attractions in our life.

Remember this…

The more you complain for what you don't have, the more you will attract the reasons to complain.
The more you are grateful for what you have, the more you will attract reasons for gratitude.

Before we go to the next technique, be grateful by saying thank you for 10 things in your life right now and check how you feel.

While gratitude is the best way to take control of your feelings, here is another superb technique.

Conscious Questions – Creating Any Emotion You Need

The quality of questions we ask ourselves creates the quality of our emotions. If you ask yourself negative questions, you create negative emotions; if you ask yourself positive questions, you create positive emotions.

In a negative situation, when you ask yourself why this always happens with you, you feel helpless and frustrated because your question leads you to these emotions.

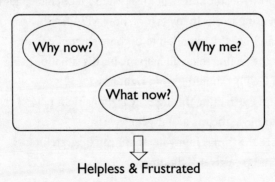

Helpless & Frustrated

But if you ask yourself how you could use the situation to become a better human being, you will feel strong and confident. If negative questions lead to negative emotions, positive questions can also lead to positive emotions.

Thus using conscious questions is an extremely powerful and guaranteed way to change your emotions.

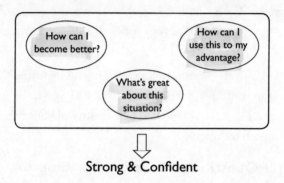

Strong & Confident

Use conscious positive questions to create positive emotional energy before unconscious negative questions create negative emotional energy.

Here is a list of 25 powerful questions I ask myself to create positive emotions:

1. What can I be excited about today?
2. How will my work help me fulfil my dreams today?
3. What positive emotions will I feel when I face challenges today?
4. If everything works in my favour, how will I feel?
5. How can I use this situation to become a better person?
6. What's the feeling that will help me in this situation?
7. Which feelings should I avoid right now?
8. What am I attracting through my feelings right now?
9. Who do I love the most in my life?
10. What are the things in my life that I can be grateful for?
11. How can I be a giver right now?

12. What good qualities in me can I focus on?
13. What great qualities may I have overlooked in my relationship/s?
14. How can I take control of my feelings right now?
15. How will I feel about this situation five years from now?
16. What feeling do I want to sleep with right now?
17. Which feeling will help me solve this problem right now?
18. How will I celebrate if I solve this problem?
19. Who are the people who love me unconditionally?
20. What are the best memories of my life?
21. What are the best memories I can create for my life?
22. What do I want to feel if this is the last day of my life?
23. What's great about life right now?
24. What can I do to make someone happy?
25. Do I want to be in control of my feelings or let them control me?

I am sure simply reading these positive questions will make you feel positive. That's because every question has a pre-supposed feeling to which it will lead.

Here is a list of negative questions that most people unconsciously use:

1. Why does this happen to me?
2. Why did this happen right now?
3. What am I going to do now?
4. What if it gets worse?
5. Why don't people understand me?
6. Why do people behave in the wrong way?
7. Why do people cheat me?
8. Why do people take me for granted?
9. How can I prove that I am right?
10. Why is life not supporting me?

11. When will this time get over?
12. Why can't they leave me alone?
13. Why do I have to do this?
14. What's the point of doing what I am doing?
15. Why can't I get what I want?
16. Why am I struggling in life?
17. What if my boss does not give me what I want?
18. What if they say 'NO'?
19. Why is it so difficult to convince this person?
20. How can I take revenge to teach him a lesson?
21. What if I fail?
22. What if it doesn't work?
23. Why is life unfair?
24. Why can't I control my feelings?
25. What if I lose control?

As you read these negative questions you will also feel the negative energy they create. Questions are like magic spells that can be used to create positive or negative feelings at any time.

Most people unconsciously or unknowingly use negative questions to feel negative and thus transmit negative energy in the universe; this in turn creates negative attractions in life.

Here is an exercise which will help you practice conscious questions and attract positive energy in your life.

Conscious Questioning Exercise:

Here is a simple three-step exercise to help you consciously use positive questions to create positive emotional frequency and thus positive attractions in your life:

1. **Recognize the negative questions** you ask yourself in those areas of your life where you attract negative results.

2. **Stop asking** these negative questions immediately.
3. **Create positive questions** that you will now use to create positive emotions and therefore generate positive attractions.

The whole idea is to take control of the frequency at which you vibrate so that you can control what you attract. During my corporate workshops sometimes participants ask me questions that interrupt the flow of my workshop. Earlier, unconsciously I used to ask myself, why do people interrupt me? Why do people ask silly questions?

Obviously such negative questions led me to negative emotions like irritation and frustration which led me to negative thoughts and negative attractions.

So I consciously recognized and wrote down all my negative questions. This was step one. Step two, I made a decision to stop asking myself any negative questions. And as step three, I even created positive questions to help me feel positive when a participant interrupted the flow of my workshop.

Here are the three positive questions I created for positive frequency attractions. How can I improve my listening skills? How can I use this as an opportunity to build trust with my participants? How can I handle questions and yet learn to maintain the flow of my workshop?

These questions helped me feel positive emotions like being creative, open and intelligent. As a result I actually became very good at handling questions in all my workshops.

Now ask yourself where in your life you are unconsciously asking yourself negative questions, recognize those negative questions, stop asking them and quickly create positive questions right now to create positive frequency attractions in your life.

Using positive questions can make you a Good Luck Magnet. If you want to attract good luck then use the following Law of Attraction technique…

Control What You Say to Control Your Attractions

**You can control the flow of your emotional energy and what
you attract by controlling what you say.**

You can either let your emotions control what you say or you can
control your emotions through what you say.

Every word you say (even casually) is sound energy with a particular
frequency. When you talk you literally transmit that energy frequency
and attract its matching frequency back to you.

Not realizing the impact of what we say, we end up saying many
negative things during our conversations with our friends, family and
colleagues. This negative talking tunes us to a negative frequency and
then we wonder why we attract problems in life.

**When I was writing this book, I unconsciously started saying
negative things to my wife like:**

- I am confused about this chapter.
- I am not sure if I am doing justice to this topic.
- I feel I am in the wrong direction.
- I am not in the mood for writing today.
- I feel like I am stuck on this chapter.

The more I said things like these, the more my ideas were blocked.

Our mind is like a CPU connected to the server of the universe where
there is access to unlimited knowledge and ideas.

When we say "I am stuck", "I don't understand", "I am confused", "I
don't know what to do", we block the connection between our mind and
the universal server. Thus we stop receiving creative ideas.

I realized that I had blocked my connection with the universal server
by saying negative things.

So after that I became conscious and whenever I would catch myself talking negative, I would say:

CANCEL – CANCEL

Remember what I said? Every word has its own energy frequency.

When we say the word 'cancel' twice, we use the frequency of this word to cancel out all the negative things we said. It's like using the 'delete' button on your computer. It actually works! Try it out.

Right now say something negative and then say 'Cancel-Cancel' and you will actually feel better after saying it.

So I would say 'Cancel-Cancel' and immediately say positive things which would help me connect back to the universal server for positive ideas.

Here is how I replaced my negative talk with positive talk with my wife:

Negative talk energy	Positive talk energy
I am confused about this chapter.	I am now clear about this chapter.
I am not sure if I am doing justice to this topic.	I am doing perfect justice to this topic.
I am confused.	I am absolutely clear now.
I feel like I am in the wrong direction.	I feel like I am in the right direction now.
I am not in the mood for writing today.	I am in the perfect mood for writing today.

I feel like I am stuck on this chapter.	I feel like I am intuitively guided while writing this chapter.

If you're as logical as I am, you are probably thinking, "Shouldn't I talk what I am really feeling? Won't I be lying to myself if I say the opposite of what I am actually feeling?"

Well! You can either use your feelings to impact what you talk or you can use what you talk to impact how you feel.

After I started using this positive talk with my wife I actually felt a surge of positive creativity which helped me write my book and I found myself more satisfied with my writing than ever before.

You must have experienced that when we sit with friends, we tend to talk negatively about the market. One person in the group may start with, "Have you seen the news today? Sensex is down again." This triggers a negative thread regarding the market – how tough it is, how difficult it is to find a job, how business opportunities are rare, how customers don't spend money, etc.

As a result, this impacts our business because we have tuned into the frequency of bad market. Thus we start attracting problems in our business.

I never agree with people when they say that the market is bad: "The market always has business for excellent companies," I say.

If you look at the history of businesses, you will realize that most millionaires grew out of recession or tough times.

How is that? Remember that negative and positive frequency is always around you, it is you who tunes into them. Similarly, problems and opportunities are always available in the market, we just need to tune into the opportunities.

A great way to tune into the frequency of opportunities is to talk more about them than about the problems.

If you talk opportunities you attract opportunities but if you talk problems you attract problems.

Here are the areas where we end up talking negatively without realizing that we are tuning into negative energy:

Areas of Life	Unconscious Negative Talk
Relationships	Sarcastic jokes about marriage
Job	Cribbing about the organization/boss
Family	These people don't understand me
Money	Market is really bad
People	It is difficult to find good people
Life	Life is not easy
Problems	It is impossible to solve this problem

It is scientifically proven through experiments that plants respond to what we talk. If you talk positive things to a plant it grows well. On the other hand, if you talk negative things to a plant, it gets affected by that negative energy and starts deteriorating.

Masaru Emoto, a scientist, conducted an experiment on the impact of words on water. He took samples of water and stored them in two different bottles. On one bottle he wrote negative words like "You are a fool" and on the second bottle he wrote "Thank you". To each bottle he would say these relevant words every day.

After a few days, when he observed the water through the microscope, he found that the water sample with negative words had a negative formation of cells whereas the water sample with positive words had formed a beautiful crystal.

Now if such was the effect of a few words on a small amount of water, then consider this: About 60 per cent of your body is made of water. When you talk negative things during the day imagine the impact it has on the water in your body. Imagine the impact it has on your health and state of mind.

I hope you have realized the power of what you talk and how it literally shapes your reality. If you have, then do the following exercise to take control of what you talk.

Exercise to Take Control of Your Talking Frequency

Now use the following table to recognize your negative talk energy and convert them into positive talk energy:

Areas of Life	Unconscious Negative Talk	Conscious Positive talk

I am sure you remember Jack who used the gratitude technique. He also used the above table to recognize and change his negative talk into positive talk frequency.

In fact, even now when I face negative attractions I use the above table to recognize and change my frequency. It's easy to use and gives you immediate results. Give it a shot!

And if you are hungry for more frequency changing techniques then continue reading about a technique which will remove more than 50 per cent of negative energy in your life and fill it with awesome positive energy.

Forgiveness and Acceptance – Release the Brakes

Imagine driving an expensive sports car with the hand brakes on. You would never get to use the full potential of this car unless you release the hand brakes.

Negative emotions like anger, hatred, regret, frustration, helplessness or any emotion which keeps you stuck in your past problems and experiences will work like hand brakes.

YES! Negative emotions are hand brakes that will slow you down; they won't allow you to use the full potential of your positive emotions to drive your life at its optimum speed.

It is critical that you release these brakes, and in order to release them, you must practice forgiveness and acceptance.

The more you keep anger, frustration, complaints the more you will attract negative energy in your life. Because anger is like poison which we drink and expect others to die.

Thus forgiveness is not for others; it is for your own sake so that you can release the energy that attracts all the unwanted negative energy in your life. Here is an example.

Despite the hard work he put in, a friend's business showed no signs of growth. One day, as we discussed the problems and what was making him attract negative problems in his business, we discovered that his hand brakes were on.

He was short-tempered and always angry with his wife when at home. During our discussion he realized that these negative emotions were blocking his ability to tune into positive emotions in his business. It was impacting his productivity and focus due to which he was unable to create the desired results.

That day he closed his eyes and mentally forgave his wife and himself for all the past fights and arguments that they had had. He decided that he would let go of the past and start afresh. After all, true love involves forgiveness. Once he started vibrating at the frequency of attracting positive energy, not only did he experience improvement in his relationship with his wife but also in his business.

Remember that we are all one at the energy level, so by directing anger towards someone else you direct it towards yourself. When you forgive others, you forgive a part of yourself in other people.

People ask me, "Is it that simple? Can I simply forgive and accept myself or someone else simply by saying so?"

And my answer is, "If anger increases by expressing, then why can't forgiveness and acceptance increase by expressing it?"

I have used this simple technique of simply closing my eyes and saying to myself, "I forgive and accept this person/situation and myself", and every time I did this I experienced an instant release of negative hand breaks and an instant flow of positive emotions.

But hey, don't believe me blindly, try it yourself right now!

All you have to do is write simple forgiveness statements, close your eyes and say it to yourself, feel it as you say it and see how your life starts changing. When you forgive people and release the negative energy from your system, you stop attracting negative things in your life and start attracting positive things because forgiveness and acceptance is a positive frequency.

And remember you are not forgiving for someone else but to release your own negative hand breaks.

So don't delay another minute and do the following forgiveness exercise...

Forgiveness Exercise

People you are angry with	Forgiveness statements

The best part is that since we are all connected at the energy level, you don't necessarily need to talk to people in person. Just close your eyes, right away, and forgive them, commit to start afresh; they will get the message energetically.

Negative emotions like frustration, irritation, helplessness also happen when people or situations don't behave the way we like. For example, you may feel frustrated about why your spouse does not understand your point of view or you may feel agitated why people break traffic rules while driving or you may feel upset about why your boss does not understand your point of view or you may feel dissatisfied with the amount of money you make, etc.

I am sure you have experienced that feeling frustrated, irritated or helpless does not change others but it makes your life hell because you are the one tuning into negative emotional energy, not them.

I follow a simple principle which helps me deal with such things:

Change what you can, accept what you can't!

I focus all my energy in areas where I can change people or situations. Where I know I cannot change the way people are or the way situations are, I simply accept them and move on. I choose to give it zero attention, zero energy.

For example, I know I can't change the way people drive so I don't give it any attention and simply focus all my energy on those things where I can change something. As a result, I am more productive and mostly tuned into positive emotions, attracting more positive energy in my life.

In fact, a root cause of stress for most people is constantly trying to change what they cannot.

Acceptance Exercise

Use the following acceptance exercise to recognize areas, people and situations that you cannot change, recognize the negative emotions you experience with them. Now write down acceptance statements to stop all the negative emotions.

People or situations that you cannot change but feel negative about	Negative emotions you experience	Acceptance statements for these areas

Now stop trying to change things in the above areas and start accepting them as they are, not because it is right or wrong to do so but because it is not worth wasting your emotional energy here.

Summary of Emotions

- E-motions are energy in motion.
- There are two types of energy frequencies: positive and negative.
- These frequencies are controlled by your emotions which are also positive and negative.
- Thus your emotions are energy vibrating at a positive or negative frequency.
- Every day, every minute you feel something, thus you transmit energy of a certain frequency in the universe to attract its matching frequency.
- Gratitude technique is a simple technique to control your emotional frequency.
- Gratitude simply means being grateful or thankful for what you have.
- Gratitude is a shortcut to all positive attractions in your life.

Gratitude exercise:

- ▶ Write down all the areas of your life where you experience negative emotion.
- ▶ Stop feeling negative in these areas.
- ▶ Thank God for what you want in that area as if you already have it.

Three gratitude practices I personally follow:

- ▶ Morning gratitude
- ▶ Night gratitude
- ▶ Frequency changing gratitude

- The more you complain about what you don't have, the more you will attract situations of lack.

- The more you are grateful for what you have, the more you will attract situations for which to be grateful.
- Another great technique to change your emotions is conscious questioning.
- The quality of questions we ask ourselves creates the quality of our emotions.
- If you ask yourself negative questions you will create negative emotions; if you ask yourself positive questions you will create positive emotions.

Conscious questioning exercise:

- ▶ Recognize the negative questions you ask yourself in those areas of your life where you have been attracting negative results.
- ▶ Stop asking these questions.
- ▶ Write a list of positive questions that you will use to create positive emotions needed to create the positive attractions you desire.

- One of the simplest techniques to control your emotions is to control what you talk.
- You can control the flow of your emotional energy by controlling the flow of your talks.
- The more you talk negative the more you tune into negative frequency in your life.
- The more you talk positive the more you tune into positive frequency in your life.
- Every time you catch yourself talking negative, stop yourself and say 'Cancel – Cancel' to stop the negative frequency.

Here is an exercise to take control of your talking frequency:

Areas of life	Unconscious negative talk	Conscious positive talk

- Negative emotions are hand brakes that will slow you down and they will not allow you to use the full potential of your positive emotions to drive your life at its optimum speed.
- Practice forgiveness and acceptance to release the hand brakes of positive emotional energy.
- You forgive people for your own sake so that you can release the energy that attracts all the unwanted stuff in your life.
- We are all one at the energy level so by directing anger towards someone else you direct it towards yourself.
- When you forgive others you forgive a part of yourself in other people.
- Feeling frustrated, irritated or helpless does not change others but it does make your life hell because you are the one tuning into negative emotional energy, not them.

The forgiveness exercise:

People you are angry with	Forgiveness statements

- Change what you can, accept what you can't.
- Stop wasting your energy on people and situations that you cannot change; accept them.

The acceptance exercise:

People or situations which you cannot change but you feel negative about	Negative emotions you experience	Write acceptance statements

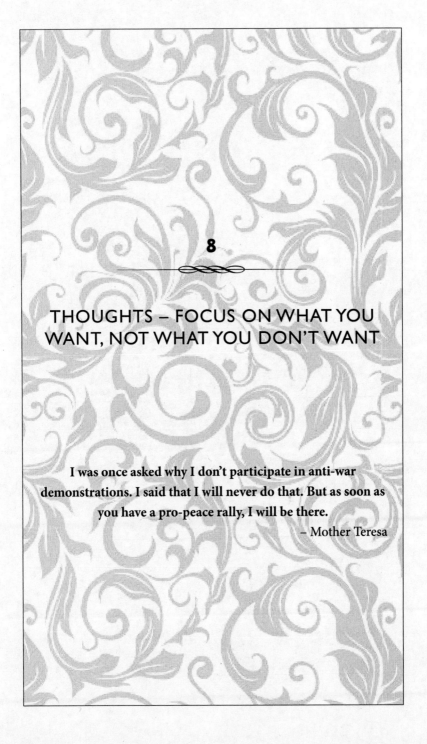

8

THOUGHTS – FOCUS ON WHAT YOU WANT, NOT WHAT YOU DON'T WANT

I was once asked why I don't participate in anti-war demonstrations. I said that I will never do that. But as soon as you have a pro-peace rally, I will be there.

– Mother Teresa

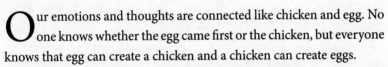

Our emotions and thoughts are connected like chicken and egg. No one knows whether the egg came first or the chicken, but everyone knows that egg can create a chicken and a chicken can create eggs.

Similarly, no one knows whether feelings come first or thoughts, but we all know that our feelings can create thoughts and our thoughts can create feelings. They are interconnected.

Do you remember playing with sand on the beach when you were a child? Separately, the particles of sand have no power but if we bring them together, we can use them to make a sand castle, a mountain, a person or just about anything we want.

Just like that our thoughts are like particles of energy. When we focus on all our thoughts and bring them together, they actually attract more energy from the universe around us and create our reality.

So if you focus your thoughts on what you want, you start getting more of it. Similarly, if you focus a lot of your thoughts on what you don't want, then you generate more of what you don't want.

The Law of Attraction, what I call the universe or what some people call God, does not question what you attract. Whatever you feel, think, believe or act will get attracted to you without exception.

So if you constantly think about what you don't want and get worried about it, the universe does not give a warning sign, like a Windows PC:

By thinking of what you don't want, you are attracting more negative energy.

Are you sure you want this?

CANCEL   OK

The universe does not interfere with your frequency (FTBAs); only you have full control over it.

Remember that the Law of Attraction is like a genie; it only says, "Your wish is my command". It will neither question your command nor ask you whether you want to change it.

Haven't you had the experience of attracting exactly what you did not want or what you were most scared of?

- You didn't want your boss to catch your mistakes but he did.
- You didn't want to fail but you did.
- You didn't want to get late but you got caught in a lot of traffic.
- You wished you wouldn't have to wait in the queue and you found a long queue.
- You feared getting in the wrong relationship and you did.
- You didn't want people to cheat you and yet you found people who did that to you.
- You didn't want to lose your temper but you did.

These experiences are not coincidences, they are your attractions. The more you resist something the more you will attract it. Why does this happen?

There are two major mistakes that people make in their way of thinking and this stops them from attracting what they want, making them instead attract what they don't want.

First Mistake

Here is the first mistake you and I make in our way of thinking:

**We think a lot about what we don't want and attract more of
the unwanted negative situations.**

The only way to tune into a frequency is to feel, think, believe and act as if you already have it.

So when you think negative, you already vibrate at the frequency of having the problem. When you are thinking about getting late, in your mind you are already late. So you are tuned into the frequency of being late. Thus, you start attracting its matching frequency in the form of people and situations that actually delay you.

When you are scared of having bad relationships, you are already tuned in to the frequency of having bad relationships and thus you attract them perfectly because like attracts like.

You cannot defy the law, it works all the time.

It is your choice whether you use this law to attract more of what you want or more of what you don't want.

**I was once asked why I don't participate in anti-war
demonstrations. I said that I will never do that. But as soon as
you have a pro-peace rally, I will be there.**
                                                    – Mother Teresa

---

A participant once shared with me how he would be always scared that colleagues would take credit for his work. That's exactly what happened! He always blamed his colleagues for it but after participating in our workshop, he understood that it was he who had attracted the situation through his own negative thoughts.

Another participant shared that the more he told his son not to bang the door, the more he banged the door. Why was that?

That's because our mind thinks in pictures. When you tell others to not do something, they picture indulging in the forbidden. In this case, the boy can picture banging the door, thus he ends up repeating the behaviour. What you need to do is tell the son to close the door softly.

Similarly, when you think you don't want to have an argument with your spouse, your mind has already pictured you arguing with your spouse, so you end up arguing even if you didn't want to. The right way to think is: "I am having a peaceful conversation with my spouse today." This is what you want to attract.

Second Mistake

> **A man is but the product of his thoughts – what he thinks, he becomes.**
>
> – Mahatma Gandhi

Another mistake people make in their thinking is that they think in the future tense. Example:

- I want a promotion.
- I want to increase profits in my business.
- I want to attract a life partner.
- I want a new house.
- I want to be on time.
- I want to be successful.
- I want…

When we repeat such statements in our mind or say them aloud while talking to people, we do not vibrate at the frequency of actually having it; according to the Law of Attraction, we will never attract such goals.

Remember attraction happens only if you are tuned into the same frequency of your goals which means thinking that you already have them. Thus when you want something, it is necessary to say it in the present tense so you can tune into its frequency.

Most often we think either in the past or future tense and that too in a negative manner. This way, unconsciously, we vibrate at the exact opposite frequency of our goals. Therefore, despite working hard, people don't get what they want.

So What Do We Do?

First, stop creating negative frequency by thinking in the past tense and future tense. Then use the best way of thinking – Affirmations.

Affirmations – Tuning Your Thought Frequency

You create your thoughts, your thoughts create your intentions and your intentions create your reality.

– Wayne Dyer

Affirmation is a great way to tune your thoughts to vibrate at the required frequency of your goals. Affirmations will help you convert all your negative thoughts into positive thoughts.

What Are Affirmations?

Affirmations are *positive statements* made in the *present tense*.

When you think of something in a positive way and in the present tense, you start vibrating at its exact matching frequency and attract it. And if you add adjectives like: "Thank you God", "I am so happy", "I am so excited now that..." These adjectives will add more positive emotions in your affirmations.

Here are some examples of how to convert your incorrect thinking into affirmations so you can start vibrating at positive frequency:

Incorrect thinking (negative or past and future statements)	Affirmations (positive and present tense statements)
1 I want to increase profits.	Thank God for increasing my profits.
2 I want a promotion.	I am so happy that I have got my desired promotion.
3 I want a life partner.	Thank you God for a loving and understanding life partner.
4 I don't want to be late.	I am so relaxed now that I have reached on time.
5 I don't want my boss to shout at me.	I am so relieved my boss spoke to me with respect.
6 I don't want problems in my relationship.	Thank God my relationship is full of love, strength and stability.
7 I don't want money problems in my career.	I am so happy that my career is full of opportunities.
8 I hope nothing goes wrong during my interview.	Thank God my interview was successful; I am so relieved and happy.
9 I hope they don't reject my proposal.	I am so thankful they have accepted my proposal.
10 What if they don't like my idea.	I am so excited that they loved my idea.
11 What if my project does not finish on time.	I am so happy and relieved that my project has completed before time.

So whenever you catch yourself thinking negatively, ask yourself these two simple questions to change your thought frequency:

1. What am I attracting by negative thinking?
2. What affirmations can I say to attract what I want?

If you truly want to attract your goals, you must affirm that you already have them in your life.

Here are a couple of stories of how affirmations can give magical results.

One of my participants, Bhupendra Rathore, wanted his sister to get married but they were unable to find a suitable groom for her. In the language of Law of Attraction, this means that they were not vibrating at the right frequency of marriage and were thus unable to attract the right person.

In a personal coaching session, we helped Bhupendra to make a list of positive affirmations based on the basic question of what he wanted for his sister. He made affirmations like:

- *I am so happy and thankful that my sister has found a very loving and understanding life partner.*
- *Thank God everybody is very happy in the marriage.*
- *I am so relieved and thankful that everything in the marriage has been taken care of perfectly within our budget.*

After writing these affirmations, he made sure that he was reading them three times a day: first thing when he gets up in the morning, during the day whenever he would feel worried about his sister's marriage and last thing before he sleeps at night.

In just a month after that, Bhupendra found the right person for his sister and the marriage took place exactly as he had written in his affirmations.

What had not happened for a long time took place immediately after he tuned into the right frequency by conditioning his FTBAs through affirmations.

Your affirmations help you feel, think, believe and act as if you have already achieved your goal. As a result, your actions start attracting positive energy in the form of people and situations that are always around you.

God helps those who help themselves.

I have been successfully using affirmations for many years to achieve my monthly business goals. I had a magical experience in the initial period of conducting workshops for small groups. I wanted large group workshops where I could address hundreds of people in a single batch.

Unconsciously, for some time I had been using the Law of Attraction against myself by saying things like: other trainers are lucky that they get large group workshops. Will I ever get large group workshops? Why don't I get large group workshops? The market does not have requirements for large group workshops.

By repeating statements like these, I was unconsciously vibrating at the wrong frequency, feeling jealous, helpless and unlucky, and hence, not attracting what I so desired. As soon as I became conscious of it, I stopped saying, thinking and feeling anything that made me feel the lack. Next, I wrote down affirmations to tune into the right frequency and repeated them three times in a day:

- *Thank God, I have got so many opportunities to conduct large group workshops now.*
- *I am feeling so satisfied and complete now that I do these large group workshops.*

- *I love the excitement of working with large groups of hundreds of people in almost every workshop I conduct nowadays.*

I started taking action with congruent and positive feelings, thoughts and beliefs to sell myself for such workshops confidently.

As a result of these affirmations, in just two months after that, I attracted my first large group workshop opportunity! I was invited to conduct a workshop for Piramal Healthcare where they wanted me to train 2500 employees in just four days. This was truly magical for me and the best part is that the magic continues as even today most of my workshops are large group interventions.

You can attract anything you want in life as long as you vibrate at its matching frequency. Sometimes people ask me, "How long will it take to attract my goals after I start using my affirmations?"

There is no fixed time for this. Different people will take different time to tune into the right frequency but I can tell you one thing, if you keep conditioning the frequency, you will tune into it one day and that day you will magically attract what you want.

Make affirmations for every area of your life. Not only to attract new goals in your life but also for areas where you would like to maintain your positive frequency. Here is a list of my personal affirmations which I use on a daily basis.

In this list I have included affirmations for my new goals and for the positive frequency that I want to maintain in my life.

| Training | – I am internationally famous as one of the best leadership trainers in the world. |
| | – I am one of the best behaviour-transformation trainers in the world. |

	– The universe constantly guides me to create instant transformations for people in all my workshops. – In all my workshops I get a 100 per cent successful rating. – Indu and I regularly travel the world in business class flights and stay in 5-Star hotels for international workshops. – I conduct workshops all over the world for thousands of people in every country I travel.
Writing books	– I am a successful author as all my books are international bestsellers. – All my audio and video products are international bestsellers and help millions of people to create amazing transformations in their life.
Finances	– Financially we are always taken care of and always live in abundance. – We are one of the biggest brands in the field of corporate training. – Our brand value is compared with that of Robin Sharma, Shiv Khera and Anthony Robbins.
Health	– I weigh 64 kgs with a 30-inch waist and a strong flat stomach with strong abs. – My biceps are 12 inches and my chest is 38 inches.

	– Physically, Indu and I are fit, healthy and full of vitality.
	– Indu and I meditate for 15 minutes and exercise for 45 minutes every day.
Relationships	– I always give abundance of love, time and money to all my family members.
	– I love and respect Indu and always show appreciation and keep the romance alive.
	– I give a lot of time to every member of the family and talk to them with love and respect.
Material possessions	– I have fully owned property assets worth 'x' crores as of today (write the date here).
Spirituality	– I practice being responsive by using the best of positive words, tone and body language.
	– I always live in the present moment and live in gratitude for whatever I already have.
	– Most importantly, I always remember that we are all one – I am one with everyone and everyone is one with me.

Every morning I start my day by loudly repeating these affirmations to myself while walking on my treadmill. Every night before I sleep I repeat these affirmations and sleep in the frequency of my perfect life.

Since the time I started using these affirmations almost all my goals are achieved in ways which are truly magical. Start creating magic in your life too by making a list of your own affirmations.

If you need support in creating affirmations, you can call for a personal coaching session by contacting us through our website.

A lot of my participants tell me that they experience magical results when they use the affirmations but the problem is that they forget to use them regularly and sometimes their positive attractions stop.

So I created the following technique to put affirmations on autopilot so they would create their positive frequency automatically. Interested in this autopilot technique? Continue reading...

Recording Affirmations

The possession of anything begins in the mind.

–Bruce Lee

This particular technique will put your affirmations on autopilot and give you superb results. It is based on the principle 'output depends on input'. What goes in your mind is what comes out of it.

If a person is told again and again that he is very bad at his work, he is bound to continue producing bad results even in the future.

When you appreciate a person and encourage them, you are giving positive inputs to their mind which in turn gives positive output after some time.

Thus a student who is poor at mathematics can improve if he is given enough positive encouragement compared to the negative input that he is bad at it. The best input in our mind happens when our subconscious is most active. Thus, when we are vulnerable, emotionally relaxed or disturbed, whatever people say to us goes deep into our subconscious.

The recording technique is made to take advantage of this principle and condition our thoughts faster than ever before.

Record affirmations to program your subconscious mind.

Most of our mobile phones have recording facilities, all you have to do is record your affirmations in your mobile recorder and put it on (loop) or repeat mode before you sleep at night. Just remember to use the lowest volume possible and put your phone on charger.

Let the phone play your affirmations beside your pillow. While you sleep, your mind will be programmed with your affirmations.

If you listen to a song ten times you can't help humming that song; imagine the effect on your mind when you play your affirmations for six hours of sleeping time.

In just a few days, your mind gets conditioned with your new affirmations and tunes into the right frequency of your goals and the attraction starts happening like magic.

Here are a couple of stories of how people have used the recording technique to create magical attraction in their life:

One of my participants was struggling with her divorce. She wanted it to be peaceful but for some reason constant misunderstandings with her husband was making things worse. When she met me, she was disturbed, sad, angry, and confused and carried a bagful of other negative emotions that were quite natural in her situation.

During our workshop she realized that as per the cycle of Law of Attraction, she may have attracted the divorce. Twenty per cent was perhaps destiny but the way she responded to the situations with her FTBAs she was bound to attract more negative situations.

She decided to stop transmitting negative energy frequencies by changing her FTBAs. One of the main techniques she used was the recording technique with her new affirmations to condition her mind with completely new and positive frequencies.

Here is a list of affirmations she recorded and listened to while she slept every night:

- *I am happy and grateful for everything that I have in life.*
- *Every challenge during my divorce is teaching me to become emotionally stronger than ever before.*
- *I am so grateful now that I have got my divorce peacefully.*
- *My ex-husband and I have completely forgiven each other.*
- *We both have made a fresh start and live happily after our divorce.*

After three months of listening to the recorded affirmations, she called me one day and said that things had improved magically in the last few months and she had successfully signed her divorce that morning. The best part was that the divorce took place peacefully. She was very happy and ready to make a fresh start, exactly as she had wanted.

Just imagine! When a person is conditioned with positive affirmations for six hours every night while asleep, it is obvious that they will start transmitting lots of positive energy which in turn will attract positive results.

A friend came to me when he experienced a huge loss of ₹40 lakh in his business. He was extremely depressed and feeling hopeless; he thought it would be impossible for him to recover from such a loss and had decided to commit suicide.

After two hours of coaching, he was clear that everything that had happened in his business was his own attraction. If he truly wanted to change his attraction he would have to make new goals and align his feelings, thoughts, beliefs and actions accordingly.

This is the list of affirmations that he made to condition his FTBAs:

- *I am so happy and grateful today that I have recovered ₹40 lakh in my business in just one year.*
- *I am so happy that I had a great relationship with my bank during this period and they were extremely supportive and patient with me.*
- *Thank you God for all the opportunities you gave me to re-establish my business and become stronger than ever before.*

He made sure he was listening to such recorded affirmations three times a day and also using the visualization technique. A week after that he called to say that he had convinced the bank to give him one year's time to return their money. As he had desired, they were very supportive and patient with him and were willing to trust him.

Exactly within the year he recovered ₹40 lakh and even made a profit of ₹10 lakh. It has been three years since then; today he is a multi-millionaire.

The Law of Attraction will never question your desires, never doubt or judge you. The Law of Attraction is a genie that simply says, "Your wish is my command".

So I hope you are inspired to start recording your affirmations right now.

Feed Yourself with Great Thoughts

We all have two powerful magnets within us – negative frequency magnet and positive frequency magnet.

Many times we give more power to the negative frequency magnet by:

- Reading negative news every day.
- Watching negative news.
- Listening and engaging in office gossip and grudges.
- Listening to sad music.
- Watching sad movies or movies with negative messages.
- Subscribing to gossip Facebook groups or pages.

With such inputs, the negative magnet becomes more and more powerful and unconsciously we start attracting a lot of negative frequency in our life.

So stop giving power to the negative magnet. In fact, start giving more power to your positive magnet by:

- Reading inspirational content in the morning.
- Watching happy movies.
- Listening to happy music.
- Engaging with people who talk about solutions, not problems.
- Reading the biography of a great leader before you go to sleep every night.
- Reading inspiring blogs.
- Subscribing to inspiring social network pages.
- Learning something productive everyday.

Remember this: The output always depends on the input. Give so many great inputs to your positive magnet that the only output possible is positive.

Feed yourself with so many strong thoughts that the weak ones have no place in your mind.

Fill up the following table to recognize the negative inputs that you will stop giving yourself and the positive inputs that you will start from today.

Negative inputs	Positive outputs

Making these small changes to your life style will make a great difference in what you attract in your life. Now let's learn about the most powerful way to change your thoughts… Change your beliefs!

Summary of Thoughts

- The relationship between emotions and thoughts is similar to the relationship between a chicken and an egg – we don't know which came first but we know that they impact each other.
- When you focus on what you want, you get more of what you want.
- When you focus on what you don't want, you get more of what you don't want.
- The Law of Attraction or the universe does not interfere with what you attract with your FTBAs.
- Without any exception, you will always attract what you feel, think, believe and act.
- Affirmations is a great technique to tune your frequency (FTBAs) to attract what you want.
- Affirmations are positive statements made in the present tense.
- After you write your affirmations read them three times in a day:

▶ First thing in the morning.
▶ Last thing at night before you sleep.
▶ Anytime during the day when you think negatively about your goals.

- For faster results, record you affirmations in your mobile phone and listen to them all night.
- Feed yourself with great thoughts.

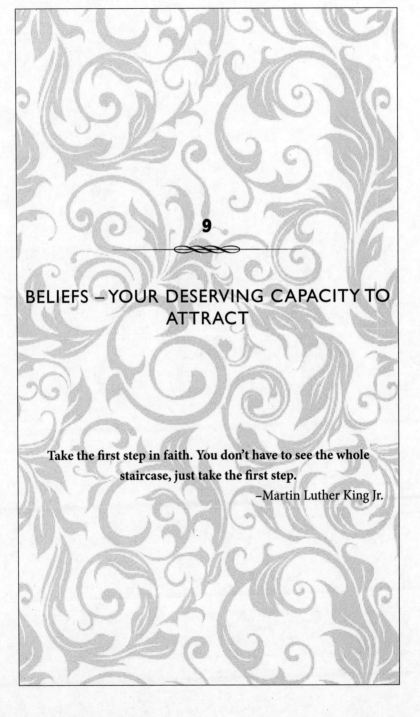

9

BELIEFS – YOUR DESERVING CAPACITY TO ATTRACT

Take the first step in faith. You don't have to see the whole
staircase, just take the first step.

–Martin Luther King Jr.

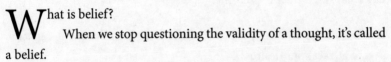

What is belief?

When we stop questioning the validity of a thought, it's called a belief.

For example, "a tree is green"; this is a belief because we never question its validity.

But what do our beliefs have to do with the Law of Attraction?

Our beliefs play the role of what we think we deserve in our life.

The Law of Attraction works in response to what we believe we deserve, not what we desire.

Have you experienced stagnation in some areas of your life? Do some problems keep repeating? Are you trying to achieve something, but keep failing despite your efforts? Do you keep experiencing bad luck in some areas?

- Trying to lose weight but not being able to.
- Wanting a good relationship but meeting the wrong person repeatedly.

- Lacking in income growth.
- Meeting people who cheat you.
- Making mistakes you don't want to.
- Developing health problems.

These are the results of your attractions based on your *Limiting Beliefs* which limit your deserving capacity to attract your desires.

I am sure there are also areas of your life where you experience growth without much effort. These are areas where your attractions are based on your beliefs called *Growing Beliefs* which help you increase your deserving capacity to attract your desires.

These are the two types of beliefs that control what you deserve and thus what you attract in your life:

1. **Limiting Beliefs** – Any belief which limits your deserving capacity to attract your desires.
2. **Growing Beliefs** – Any belief which helps you increase your deserving capacity to attract your desires.

So for example, if you believe that it is difficult to lose weight, then your subconscious believes that you deserve to be overweight even though you consciously desire to lose weight. Here is a metaphor to understand this.

Imagine you are tied to a pole with a rope and you're trying to move forward. What happens?

The pole will restrict your movement. It will not allow you to move forward towards your desires. Consider this pole as your limiting belief which says that you don't deserve to move beyond this point because it is difficult to lose weight.

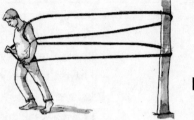

I can't lose weight!

Limiting beliefs like these restrict your actions and therefore constrain you from tuning into the right frequency of your desires.

Just like this, we have many limiting beliefs that limit our actions and thus limit our growth.

> **To attract what you want you must increase
> your deserving capacity by converting your limiting beliefs
> into growing beliefs.**

As you read this, try and recognize the areas of your life where you think your growth is limited because of your limiting beliefs, beliefs that restrict your deserving capacity.

Here are some more examples of limiting beliefs in different areas of life:

Areas of life	Limiting Beliefs
Life	– Life is not fair.
	– Life is complicated.
	– Life is difficult.
	– I am very unlucky in life.

Health	– It is difficult to lose weight. – Everybody cannot lose weight. – I have a tendency to gain weight. – I have a tendency to get health issues. – I have a weak immune system since childhood.
Emotions	– I can't control my temper, that's the way I am. – I get depressed when I see people hurt. – I cannot say "NO". – I can't handle conflicts.
Money	– Money is the cause of all the problems in the world. – Money is not important. – Money cannot buy happiness. – I don't need money. – It's difficult to make money. – Not everyone can be rich. – Rich people cannot be truly happy.
Relationships	– People cannot be trusted. – I always get the wrong people in my life. – It's not easy to manage relationships. – Relationships get stale as they get old. – It's not possible to have romance after many years of marriage.

	– Marriage is a burden.
	– Marriage is a big risk.
Career	– Work is boring.
	– It is difficult to grow fast in a job.
	– It is difficult to start a business.

Years ago, when I was struggling, I realized that I had limiting beliefs such as, it is difficult to make money. So even though my desire was to make money effortlessly, I used to always struggle to make money.

The day I changed my beliefs, I upgraded my deserving capacity in alignment with my desires. Thus not only did my income grow but it also grew effortlessly. The best way to check your beliefs (your deserving capacity) in any area of your life is to check the attractions happening in that area.

For example, a friend of mine was not getting married for many years. When she attended my Law of Attraction workshop, she realized that she had limiting beliefs like marriage is a risk. Thus she was unable to tune into the frequency of meeting the right guy.

Within a month of changing her belief, she got into a relationship with a wonderful person. The frequency of the right person was always around her; all she had to do was tune into it.

They got married after a few months. It's been four years since then, they have a very happy and successful married life.

The bottom line is that our beliefs control what we deserve in life. Limiting beliefs limit our deserving capacity while growing beliefs improve our deserving capacity.

Rich businessmen like Bill Gates are rich because they believe they deserve to have billions. Famous actors like Shahrukh Khan are super stars because they believe that they deserve to be super stars.

While many people have the desire to be rich and famous, only a few believe they deserve to have it.

Consider our belief is like a thermostat of an air-conditioner. You have set the temperature at 22 degree Celsius but the external environment increases to 25 degree Celsius; the thermostat sends a message to the air-conditioner to work harder to control the room temperature to 22 degree Celsius as per your instructions.

Similarly, if the external environment decreases to 18 degree Celsius again the thermostat will send a message to the air-conditioner to work harder to control the room temperature to 22 degree Celsius.

Exactly like that, let's consider that a person subconsciously believes that he deserves to make ₹10,000 per month; consider this as his thermostat setting. However, he desires to make ₹20,000 per month, so he works hard to get more opportunities.

Now, the moment his external life gives him an opportunity to make ₹20,000, his thermostat will work harder to sabotage those opportunities so that he can continue to make ₹10,000 as per his set point.

At the same time, let's say there are some major problems in his career and his external life situations reduce his income to ₹5,000 per month. Again his thermostat (his beliefs) will work harder to help him grow and attract opportunities to once again make ₹10,000 as per his set point.

Similarly if a person's thermostat (belief) is set to being unhealthy, then no matter how much you help them, their subconscious will work hard to make them unhealthy as per their set point. If a person's thermostat (belief) is set to being healthy then even in the most negative environment their subconscious will work hard to keep them healthy as per their set point.

If a person's thermostat (belief) is set to having bad relationships then even though they may meet the best of people, their subconscious will work hard to sabotage their relationships as per their set point to have bad relationships. But if a person's thermostat is set to having good relationships then even though they may meet difficult people, their subconscious mind will help them improve their relationships as per their set point.

So if you really want to attract your desires, you must first change the thermostat setting – your limiting beliefs to growing beliefs.

I am sure now you are wondering how to transform your limiting beliefs into growing beliefs. Well, as usual, here is an exercise to help you do that effectively.

Changing Your Belief Set Point

Follow these simple steps to transform your limiting beliefs into growing beliefs:

1. Recognize your limiting beliefs.
2. Recognize the actions which reinforce the limiting belief and stop them.
3. Write new growing beliefs as per the rules of affirmations to replace the old limiting beliefs.
4. Write new actions required to reinforce the growing beliefs and practice them everyday.
5. Say the new belief aloud 10 times in the morning and at night before you sleep (better yet, record it and let it play all night).
6. Find references where people have these growing beliefs and their required actions.

Let me share with you how I used the above steps to change my own belief set point from limiting to growing.

I had a limiting belief that my relationships don't last, no matter how hard I tried to be good at it. Due to this set point in my beliefs I always used to break up in my relationships.

After learning about limiting beliefs, I realized that subconsciously I did not deserve to have a long term relationship, I realized I had to change my set point from the limiting belief of "My relationships don't last" to a growing belief, "I have great relationships".

So I wrote the following limiting beliefs and actions which I decided to stop immediately:

Limiting Beliefs	Limiting Actions
Relationships don't last long.	Try to avoid relationships in fear or fear being in one after a few months.
Marriage is like a cage.	Avoid giving commitment to marriage.
Girls are too demanding.	Get irritated on expectations, not respecting the girl.
Girls don't understand boys.	Try to dominate the girl as per my point of view.

With such limiting beliefs and actions it wasn't very surprising that my relationships did not last.

Here are the new growing beliefs which I created using the rules of affirmations:

Growing Beliefs	Growing Actions
Relationships are meant to last forever; mine always do.	Get into a relationship when I have the chance and be confident that it will last forever.
Marriage is a partnership.	Happily commit for marriage and treat my wife like a partner.
Girls have high expectations from men and help them see their own potential.	Be willing to change as per her expectations and give her the respect for helping me change and become a better man.
My girl understands me best.	Listen to her and understand her point of view knowing she always understands mine.

I started saying these new growing beliefs 10 times in the morning and night and prepared myself mentally to act accordingly in my new relationship.

I also applied the final step by finding friends who had similar beliefs, actions and had attracted their desired life partner.

As a result, in a very short time after that, I attracted my wife Indu. Remember that the universe will always give you what you believe you deserve, not what you desire.

Now it's your turn. Recognize your limiting beliefs in all those areas of your life where you feel stuck. Then use the above steps to change your belief set point to change your frequency and your attractions.

Summary of Beliefs

- Any thought which we don't question or doubt is called a belief.
- The Law of Attraction works in response to what we think we deserve, not what we desire.
- There are two types of beliefs.

  ▶ Limiting beliefs which limit your deserving capacity to attract your desires.
  ▶ Growing beliefs which help you increase your deserving capacity to attract your desires.

- Our beliefs are like thermostats controlling what we deserve.
- If we have limiting beliefs, our inner thermostat will work hard to limit us.
- If we have growing beliefs our thermostat will work hard to help us grow.
- If you really want to attract your desires, you must transform all your limiting beliefs into growing beliefs.

- Use the steps to change your belief set point.

  - ▶ Recognize your limiting beliefs.
  - ▶ Write down the actions which reinforce the limiting beliefs and curb them.
  - ▶ Write down new growing beliefs as per the rules of affirmations to replace the old limiting beliefs.
  - ▶ Write down new actions required to reinforce the growing belief and practice them everyday.
  - ▶ Say the new belief loudly 10 times first thing in the morning and at night before you sleep (better yet record it and let it play all night).
  - ▶ Find references where people have these growing beliefs and their required actions.

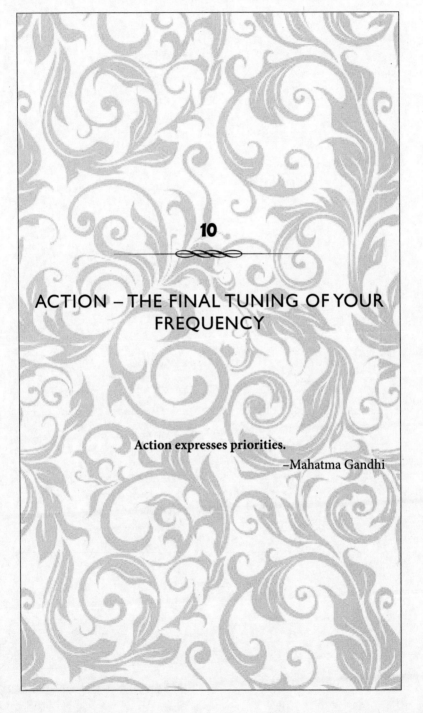

10

ACTION – THE FINAL TUNING OF YOUR FREQUENCY

Action expresses priorities.

–Mahatma Gandhi

You can attract your goals like magnets if you are willing to take action to achieve them. Your actions prove to the universe that you are serious about what you want.

Action expresses priorities.

–Mahatma Gandhi

You have probably heard this story already but I'll remind you anyway because it's a wonderful story to understand the importance of action in the Law of Attraction.

A guy started practicing the Law of Attraction with every possible technique in order to win a million dollars through lottery. He felt as if he had already won the ticket, he thought positively and never got worried, he even believed strongly that he would definitely win the ticket.

Yet he did not win the ticket! When he died, he asked the universe (God), "Even though I tuned into the exact frequency by feeling, thinking and believing as if I already have it, why didn't you give me what I wanted?"

God replied, "I would have given it to you, but you forgot to take action and buy the lottery ticket!"

A lot of people go through this experience. They try every Law of Attraction technique but are unable to get what they want. Well, it's because they are not taking enough action to tune into the right frequency.

Only when you take clear and confident action, as if you have already achieved your goal, do you attract your goals.

To attract massive results you must take massive action because the quality of your results will always depend on the quality of the actions that you take.

When you start taking clear and confident action, you give a final confirmation to the universe, I really want this and I am acting to make sure I have it. That's when your frequency is complete and you start attracting what you want. When you take action to move towards your results, they start moving towards you too.

Add Positive Value to Attract Positive Results

I want you to know that using the Law of Attraction for winning a lottery may not work most of the time because...

You get money in exchange for the 'value' you add through your actions, i.e., your services or products. The better the quality of your (actions) service or products, the more money you can demand for them. The more number of people you add value to with your (actions) services or products, the more money you will make.

You can have everything in life that you want if you just give enough other people what they want.

–Zig Ziglar

When you buy a lottery, you haven't really added any value to anybody so you cannot expect anything in return. The same is true of things like gambling, stealing, cheating, etc.

In fact, when you try to make money at the cost of other people, i.e., when you make money through gambling, stealing, cheating, lottery, you are making money at the cost of someone else's happiness. Someone gets hurt, loses money or someone feels bad.

If your money comes by making somebody else unhappy, it will not serve you well. That money will eventually attract negative energy for you in some form or the other. Either someone will cheat you, or an accident will happen or a health issue will appear where you will lose a lot of money in hospitals.

Something negative will happen because the money came with negative energy which will attract only negative frequency. Makes sense! Again, this is not about superstition. It is scientific.

When you make someone else unhappy you make yourself unhappy because at the energy level you hurt your own energy.

Similarly, if you add value through your actions and make money by making others happy, this money will bring you a lot of positive energy.

No wonder companies like Starbucks grow everywhere they go. They not only add value through excellent coffee but also through excellent customer service.

Here is a list of examples to show how this can be applied to any area of your life:

Career – Take action and be excellent at what you do to attract excellent results.

Relationships – Express your love, gratitude and affection by spending quality time with the people whom you truly value.

Money – Save money to attract more money.

Being a bestselling author – Write regularly, publish and then do everything to sell regularly.

Want to lose weight – Make sure you follow a diet plan, eat healthy and exercise regularly.

Want a new job – Keep giving interviews until you get a new job.

Want to start a business – Take the risk and invest money and start small to become big.

Want to de-stress yourself – Take action to meditate and relax.

You cannot attract results in an area where your action frequency does not match your desired results.

Here is another powerful way to use your actions to attract your goals.

Act as if you already have it!

This is the most important action technique required to tune into the exact frequency of your goals. Act as if you already have your goals or as if you are sure you are bound to achieve your goal.

For example, a woman once came to my Law of Attraction workshop; she had read a lot of books on the Law of Attraction and had applied many different techniques, but she was not able to attract a life partner.

I asked her whether she had already bought her wedding dress.

She had not.

Then I asked her the following questions:

Have you done some jewellery shopping for your marriage?
No

Have you started losing weight considering your marriage is in a month?
No

Have you done some research on where would you like to go for your honeymoon?
No

Have you decided what gift you will give your husband?
No

Have you decided how much money you will spend on your wedding?
No

Have you started saving money for your wedding expenses?
No

Have you made a list of friends and family you want to invite for your wedding?
No

When I asked her why she hadn't done any of this, she said that she would do everything when she found the right partner and her marriage date was fixed.

"Why won't you do these things before you meet the right guy? Or before your marriage date is fixed?" I asked her.

"What if I don't find the right guy or what if I find the right guy but he is not ready for marriage? What's the point in preparing for a disappointment?"

What do you think is the frequency of her actions? Marriage or difficulty in marriage?

I am sure you have recognized that her current frequency is difficulty in marriage which is exactly what she was experiencing and attracting.

When she realized this, she was shocked to know that she was the one blocking the frequency of marriage in her life.

"So what do I do now?" she asked.

The answer was simple.

Act as if you have already found your life partner and your marriage date is already fixed. Act as if you are sure you are bound to have the right guy who is just waiting to get married to you.

When all your feelings, thoughts, beliefs and actions are congruent and transmit this frequency of marriage, you will attract the right person for you.

In India, where arranged marriage is still common, this is the usual trend for parents. They start preparing the jewellery, clothes, money, look for the venue for marriage, make a list of guests, etc. Thus it is easy for them to attract the right guy for their daughter; they have been preparing for him.

Those who prepare to win are victorious.
Those who don't prepare, lose.

Here is a list of examples of how you may act to tune in to the exact frequency of your goals:

Running a restaurant – Create more space in your restaurant to have more customers. If you have more space, you create the frequency to attract more customers.

Marriage – Prepare as if your marriage date is fixed.

Being rich – Adopt the good habits of rich people and act as if you are already rich by taking calculated risks, by being proactive, by saving money regularly.

Winning a game – Work hard like a champion; book a venue for your celebration party in advance.

Be careful of all the actions you take on a daily basis, check if your actions are preparing for success or failure.

A friend of mine was cheating his organization by submitting false medical bills to make some money from his medical benefits. I asked him whether he would do the same if he were already very rich. He was categorical that he would not.

He was desperate and doing whatever was possible to make money. I explained to him that by such actions he was vibrating at the frequency of a poor person and thus he would always attract poverty, not abundance.

He understood what I was saying and started behaving as if he were already rich. He stopped cheating for money and started working with a lot of ownership in his job, behaving as if he was the owner of the company.

As a result, that year he got a promotion that he hadn't gotten in a long time. This is how our actions tune us into a certain frequency and attract it back to us.

I was once in Philippines doing a leadership workshop. We got news that a huge typhoon was going to hit Philippines on the day of our scheduled flight back to India. There were chances of not only our flight being cancelled but also of us being stuck there for a few more days.

Indu and I did our visualization and packed our bags. We acted as if we were sure to go back to India on time. A day before our scheduled flight, I was in the workshop at about 11AM. My client said that the Philippines government would probably declare all business functions closed in a few hours.

So they suggested that we stop the workshop right away and catch the same day's flight instead of waiting until the next day. We did exactly that and as a result reached India much before our scheduled arrival time.

I believe the Law of Attraction played a big role in the coincidences that happened to re-schedule our flight a day in advance. But if we had not packed our bags and were instead tense all the time about missing our flight, our actions would have transmitted the frequency of negativity. Without doubt, we could have attracted something negative.

Now it's your turn to take advantage of the Law of Attraction by doing the following exercise to tune your action frequency to your goals perfectly.

Action Tuning Exercise:

> To be a great champion, you must believe you are the best. If
> you're not, pretend you are.
>
> –Muhammad Ali

Fill in the following table to make a list of actions to act as if you already have what you want:

Goals you want to attract

_____

_____

_____

_____

_____

_____

Required action to create the 'act as if' frequency

_____

_____

_____

_____

_____

_____

Summary of Action

- To attract great results you need to take great action.
- Only when you take clear and confident action, behaving as if you have already achieved your goal, can you attract your goals.
- Add positive value to attract positive results.
- The quality of results you attract depends on the quality of your actions.
- You cannot attract results in an area where your action frequency does not match your desired results.
- So take action as if you know that you are bound to succeed and that the action is just a required formality to tune into your frequency.
- Use the action tuning exercise to figure out what action you need to take to tune your frequency to 'attracting your goals'.

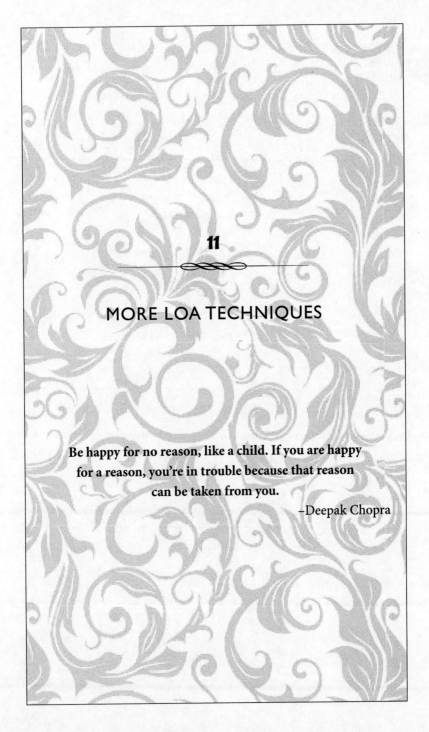

11

MORE LOA TECHNIQUES

Be happy for no reason, like a child. If you are happy
for a reason, you're in trouble because that reason
can be taken from you.

–Deepak Chopra

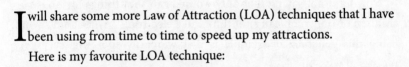

I will share some more Law of Attraction (LOA) techniques that I have been using from time to time to speed up my attractions.

Here is my favourite LOA technique:

Keep Writing Your Goals

The moment you write your goals as if you already have them, you send a magnetic energy to attract them to you.

Have you ever experienced the difficulty of finding a product in the market and then, once you buy it, suddenly you can see that product at many places. And then you wonder why you couldn't find it when you needed it the most!

This is a very common experience. Are you curious about why this happens?

It is because our brain has a part called RAS or Reticular Activating System. Whenever you associate some person or something as 'yours', the RAS gives it a high priority.

The RAS keeps scanning your environment, just like a radar, and the moment it finds the same or a similar person or product, it gives you high alert attention and that's how you spot it.

For example, a friend tells you his or her mobile number but you seem to forget it easily. But when you get a new mobile number for yourself, you seem to remember this number with very little effort. That's because the moment you say this number is yours, the RAS keeps it in a special and high priority memory bank.

Similarly, when you go for shopping, you will see that women can easily spot things that need to be bought for the house or for their children. On the other hand, men easily spot things like electronics or books to read.

Now I am not saying that only women can spot things for house or children or only men can spot things like electronics; what I am saying using this generalized example is that we easily spot whatever gets registered with our RAS.

You could use the strength of the RAS like a radar to scan for opportunities for your goal. It is very easy to use the RAS. All you have to do is write something down and the RAS knows this is important and will give it high priority; the RAS will keep scanning for it everywhere and give you a high alert the moment it finds it.

That is why in school we were asked to write those things which we needed to remember. Makes sense now!

Now the trick here is to write as if you already have the goal because then the RAS believes this is yours, it is important and it will give you a high alert attention the moment it finds some person or something related to it.

For example, I once trained an organization of 200 people who were unable to meet their goals for about six months. I asked all of them to write a reminder in their mobile –"Congratulations! We have already achieved ₹250 crore this financial year successfully and easily."

I asked them to play this as a daily reminder in their mobile calendar twice a day, morning and evening. I also asked them to write this statement repeatedly whenever they could during the day while at work.

Some of them even started writing it on paper napkins in restaurants while waiting for someone. Some of them made it a habit to write it once every day when they started their work.

As a result, that financial year they made ₹245 crore. Do you think they were upset about being short of ₹5 crore? Sure, just a little. But they were more excited about reaching ₹245 crore because they were nowhere close to their targets before this. How did this happen? When they wrote it every day, their RAS constantly scanned their environment for opportunities to meet their goal. Things which they were unable to spot earlier became clear and visible.

I regularly use the power of RAS when I go for meetings. I write my goal as – "I am able to speak confidently and creatively and have successfully got a long term business contract with this client."

Now my RAS is at work and gives me every information necessary from my subconscious memory, scans and brings my attention to every little detail the client says to help me achieve my sale. But don't just believe me blindly. Try out the power of your own RAS, write down your goal right now and add a repeat reminder in your calendar twice a day.

Keep writing this goal as if you already have it and the RAS knows this is yours already, this is important to you.

Your RAS will literally attract your attention to whatever is required to meet your goals. Try it now! Write your goal as if you already have it, right now!

Create a Vision Board

A picture speaks a thousand words.

We learnt in Chapter 9 that our mind thinks in pictures. One of the best ways to use this strength to your advantage is to create a vision board.

A vision board is a board where you display visual photographs of your goal already achieved. Go for a test drive of a car you want to buy and take a picture while sitting in the driving seat. Display this picture on your vision board.

Go to see a sample flat of your dream house, take a picture with your family in it and display that picture on your vision board.

I wanted to be a bestselling author, so I went to a shop that sells award trophies and took a photograph holding a trophy. I displayed that picture on my vision board and wrote over there, "Mitesh Khatri receiving National Bestselling Author Award".

If you want to make a certain amount of monthly income in your business, then write a cheque to yourself for that amount and display that check on your vision board.

If you want to get married, then get a beautiful wedding card and display it on your vision board with your name and add your life partner's name or a nickname that you would like to call them by.

If a friend is angry with you and you want to mend your relationship with that friend, then take a photograph of a happy memory with your friend and display it on your vision board.

If you want to lose weight, then get a photo from Google images of any model with the kind of body you desire, cut out the face and add your face to their photo. Display it on your vision board.

This is necessary because your mind can only help you achieve that which it can imagine. The more vivid and real the pictures, the more your mind gets used to the pictures, the more it will attract opportunities to make it real.

Your reality in the external world is a reflection of the reality in your internal world. I said the 'reality' of your internal world. View your vision board regularly so that the pictures of your vision board become a reality of the internal world of your mind.

Surrender – Don't Ask "How?"

**Surrender your worries, let go of your attachments and you
will realize that you are always taken care of.**

Many times participants call me after the LOA workshop or coaching
and complain that despite doing their affirmations and visualizations
every day, they are unable to get results.

"What do you feel and think most of the time about your goal?" I ask
them.

Within a few minutes of interaction, I realize that they are always
restless and constantly think about when they will attract their results
and how it will really work.

Evidently, they live in the frequency of not having the goal. How can
they attract 93.5 MHz if they are tuned into 101.5 MHz?

So I ask participants to practice surrender and stop asking how. Every
time you worry about your results, you wonder how it will happen or
get impatient. By feeling this, you block your ability to receive what you
want.

When you worry about the results, you vibrate at a negative frequency
which takes you away from your goals by attracting all kinds of negative
problems.

So stop asking how and feel, think, believe and act as if you already
have it. When you go to a restaurant and order food, do you constantly
worry about whether the food will come or not, whether the waiters or
the cook will remember your order among so many people?

No, you don't do this. You simply place the order and wait patiently.
Sometimes there is delay but eventually you get what you want.

Here is how I practiced surrender and stopped asking how. When
our first book *Awaken the Leader in You* was published, Indu and I were
initially quite confused and worried about how we could turn it into a
bestseller.

Then one day we realized that we were blocking our attraction by worrying and thinking too much about how it would happen.

So we decided that every time we thought of how, we would say, that's none of our business, the universe will take care of the how and we would just focus on taking the best possible actions that we could think of.

In just a few days after that we attracted the good fortune of meeting the bestselling author Radhakrishna Pillai, the author of *Corporate Chanakya*. He was very generous in sharing with us a lot of simple strategies that he had personally used to turn *Corporate Chanakya* and all his following books into bestsellers.

Based on his guidance, the support of our publisher (Jaico), and with the grace of the universe, we started taking the right steps and eventually in just a few months *Awaken the Leader in You* became a bestseller.

Initially, we were restless and constantly worried, so we did not attract the right frequency that would help us do the right things or have the right ideas to promote the book. However, the moment we shifted our frequency by practicing surrender and stopped asking "How?", we attracted the right people, right situations and our actions started producing results. Such is the power of surrender!

You must remember that the LOA is a world of magic, not a world of logic. If you ask "How?", you have shifted out of the world of magic and then the LOA will not work for you.

Magic happens to those who believe in it, so if you want magical results then don't ask how. Simply visualize your goal, feel grateful as if you already have it, use affirmative thoughts, believe that you deserve it, act as if you already have it and then just surrender. Let the magic happen.

The Perfect Zone

One of the ways to speed up your attraction is to live in the perfect zone instead of the imperfect zone.

For example, when we are about to go for a holiday, a few days before the date for travel we exist in a holiday zone. We are happy, excited, preparing for and looking forward to the holiday.

So you live in the holiday zone until the time you come back from your holiday. The moment you come back, you are out of the holiday state of mind.

We always live in one zone or another, one state of mind or another. When it comes to achieving goals, most people live in the imperfect zone where they feel something is missing before they achieve their goal.

Living in the imperfect zone tunes you into negative frequency and thus pushes you away from your goal. Living in the perfect zone helps you tune into the exact frequency of your goal and helps you attract it towards you.

What exactly is a perfect zone? Well, as the name suggests, it is a zone where life is perfect. Nothing is missing; everything is exactly the way you want your life to be.

Perfect zone is a state of mind where life is perfect!

Most people sleep in the imperfect zone where they believe their life is not the way it is supposed to be.

They sleep thinking, planning and wondering how to achieve their goals. Many people even have sleepless nights, worried about what will happen if they don't achieve their goals. This is the frequency of an imperfect zone.

Here is what I do when I sleep every night. I sleep imagining that my life is perfect, it is exactly the way I want it. Everything I wanted is already in my life and I do this by consciously imagining all that I want as if I already have it. I feel grateful and blessed about such a perfect life and sleep in my perfect zone.

Even though my day may have been full of challenges and barriers, I sleep in my perfect zone every night; this helps me tune in to the exact frequency of my goals to attract them towards me rather than deflect them.

Even during the day, whenever I am worried or wonder how things will work, I consciously remind myself to switch from the imperfect zone to the perfect zone.

All I do is imagine that everything is perfect and suddenly my emotions, thoughts and beliefs shift into the positive frequency.

When you live in the perfect zone, you feel secure, grounded and peaceful. As a result, you think in a positive, creative and powerful way, you have growing beliefs instead of limiting beliefs. Finally, as a result of all this, you are guided by your subconscious mind to take the right actions, creative actions and consistent actions to attract your desired results.

So starting now, create your own perfect world and live in it all the time; especially, sleep in it.

Collect Positive References

A friend of mine had been unable to achieve his business target for a long time. I asked him to use the Law of Attraction techniques like visualization and affirmations.

He refused because he thought the Law of Attraction did not work. I sat with him for an hour and helped him recognize that whenever he got results in his life, it was because he was unconsciously using the Law of Attraction by feeling, thinking, believing and acting confidently.

When he realized that the Law of Attraction is not some external force but an internal force which is always at work within us, he was willing to consciously use LOA techniques. As a result, that month he managed to achieve his business target after a very long time.

What I did with my friend was help him recognize positive references of how the Law of Attraction had already given him positive results and that too, by using it unconsciously.

When he collected positive references his ability to attract and achieve his target became faster and stronger than ever before.

When my business suffered, Indu and I were worried and started to unconsciously live in the imperfect zone regarding our business.

One day, Indu suggested that we sit and write down all those positive references in the past where we attracted the right amount of business.

In a 30-minute discussion we were able to collect more than 10 references where we were able to attract our business goals successfully. As a result, our belief that we have always been taken care of was reinforced and we were able to switch back to a positive frequency which helped us attract our goals once again.

Now, I would like you to collect at least 10 positive references of how the Law of Attraction has already worked for you so you can speed up your ability to attract more in the future.

In fact, always keep writing every positive reference of the Law of Attraction so that your beliefs are always more powerful than your doubts.

Ordinary people have more negative references of why things won't work; extraordinary people have more references related to why things will work.

To collect positive references of the Law of Attraction you can also search for the Law of Attraction results on Google, YouTube and read more books to increase your belief in this method.

Unconditional Happiness – Be Happy For No Reason

Be happy for no reason, like a child. If you are happy for a reason, you're in trouble because that reason can be taken from you.

– Deepak Chopra

You must have heard of unconditional love. Similarly, there is also something called unconditional happiness – feeling happy for no reason.

Happy people will definitely attract more happiness, so create a habit of unconditional happiness.

Unfortunately, most people practice unconditional sadness and feel sad for no reason. I am sure you have also gone through a situation where you felt low though you didn't have a concrete reason to feel so. When we are sad for any reason or even without reason, we are already vibrating at a negative frequency ready to attract more negativity.

Similarly, whether we are happy for a reason or without reason we are already vibrating at a positive frequency to attract more positivity.

All spiritual teachers promote this habit of unconditional happiness because they know that happy people attract a happy life no matter what their life conditions.

Meet LOA Practitioners

Professors meet professors, businessmen meet businessmen to enhance their knowledge and experience of their own field.

One of the best ways to become a master at using the LOA techniques is to meet more and more LOA practitioners to exchange knowledge and experience.

I have created a LOA group on Facebook where you can meet people like us and discuss your challenges, ask for solutions, share your success stories and help each other to become a better LOA practitioner.

Here is the link to your Law of Attraction facebook group: https://www.facebook.com/groups/MiraclesTM/

The Law of Attraction Coaching

One way to learn and master something is through your own experience of trial and error. Another way of learning something faster is by using someone else's experience.

Thus I encourage you to call me for a coaching session on the Law of Attraction so that you can take advantage of the years of experience that I have to help you attract your goals faster than doing trial and error.

For more LOA coaching you can contact me at mitesh@ guidinglightindia.com

Stop Using LOA

Many times when participants come to me worried that they are not able to use the Law of Attraction effectively, I advise them to stop using LOA completely for some time.

Why? Because sometimes we are tired of failing and it is critical to take a break, take some rest and then start the game after sometime.

What I mean is, there is no hurry. The Law of Attraction is not a scarce commodity. So take a break and you can start visualizing, using affirmations and taking the right actions after the break.

I do this whenever I feel uncomfortable while using LOA. As a result, my mind gets the time to relax and when I start after a few days again, my mind supports me fully. The best part about this technique is you don't have to do anything, just stop using LOA for a few days until you feel comfortable.

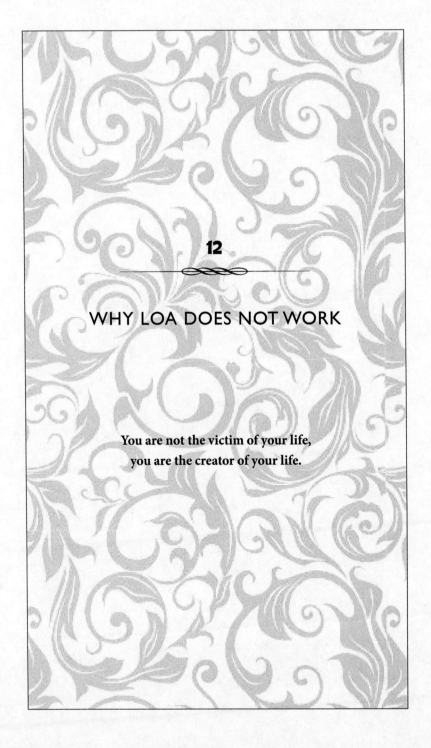

12

WHY LOA DOES NOT WORK

You are not the victim of your life,
you are the creator of your life.

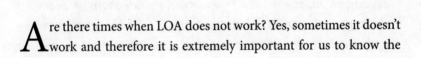

Are there times when LOA does not work? Yes, sometimes it doesn't work and therefore it is extremely important for us to know the reason for it.

There are two reasons why LOA may not work:

1. You block the frequency of your goals.
2. You are destined for something else.

Now the first reason is pretty scientific. If you are unable to attract what you want, you are definitely blocking the frequency of your goals. You are not using the Law of Attraction techniques correctly to perfectly tune into the exact frequency of your goals.

How We Block Frequency

Here are some of the ways in which we block the frequency of our desired goals and how we can unblock it:

Constant worrying – If you are constantly worried or think negatively about your goals, you definitely block the right frequency. Go back to Chapter 8 on feelings and re-learn how to manage your emotions.

Here is the story of the general manager of a multinational organization and how he realized he was blocking his own frequency. In this story, he also shares how he changed his frequency and got exactly what he wanted.

Almost six months ago, my boss gave me some feedback on my performance with many negative points. I started thinking that I was not fit for the job and I would not get further opportunities to grow in my job.

I started working towards improvements and my mind was continuously filled with the thought that I needed to improve. For almost four months, I lived in anxiety, every day facing different challenges and worries about my career. This further affected my work performance. I felt more and more stressed out every day and this had a negative impact on my personal relationships.

I met Mitesh on 5th September 2014. By that time, I had been living daily with worries, anxieties, continuously convincing my boss that I was improving. He was not happy with my performance. I knew something would go wrong drastically but I didn't know what to do.

I started practicing the Law of Attraction from the instance I met Mitesh and after attending his Law of Attraction workshop.

I started visualizing that I had successfully cleared two job interviews and that I had two jobs to choose from.

Nothing happened for a few weeks and I was getting worried that LOA was not for me.

I called Mitesh one day and told him that it was not working for me. I asked him to tell me what was wrong with me and what I needed to change in my practice.

Mitesh made me realize that even though I was visualizing my goals every day, I was blocking my own frequency by constantly being worried about when I would get a new job!

He made me realize that in order for me to tune into the frequency of my goal, I had to live my life as peacefully as if I had already cleared two interviews successfully.

On the phone Mitesh made me practice lots of gratitude for having two job options and told me to combine visualization with lots of gratitude every day.

Believe it or not, within two months I had two job offers in my hand with 30 per cent salary increase and a better profile in the exact domain where I wanted to pursue my career.

I am grateful to Mitesh and Indu Khatri for teaching me this powerful law of the universe, the Law of Attraction.

I continue to practice the Law of Attraction technique everyday to tune in to the exact frequency of my personal and professional goals. Now I know that my actions are supported with good luck which I am creating with my own feelings, thoughts, beliefs and actions.

Vasant Kale

Lack of belief – In Chapter 11, we learnt that our beliefs determine our sense of deserving. So if our belief is weak and our doubt is strong then we will have a low sense of deserving. As a result, we will definitely block the frequency of our goals. So go back to the Chapter 11 and re-learn how to change your beliefs.

Before publishing my first book, *Awaken the Leader in You,* I had increased my financial goals by 50 per cent for the year 2012. Half the year was over and I hadn't succeeded in reaching even my monthly milestones.

Whenever I realize that I am not attracting what I want, Indu and I discuss how we may be blocking our frequency and then we analyze the problems in all the four elements of our frequency – feelings, thoughts, beliefs and actions.

In the course of our discussion, we realized that we were doing our visualization exercise every morning and night, we were feeling great by practicing gratitude every day without any complaints, we were focusing on the positive outcome and had very little or no negative thoughts. We were even taking all the actions required to achieve our goals. So then what was blocking our frequency?

Suddenly Indu made me realize that I had the limiting belief that for my income to grow by 50 per cent, I had to first publish my book. I realized that I strongly believed that to grow my training business I had to take the support of publishing my book and make it a bestseller first.

I argued with her for quite some time that having a book was essential to achieving high financial goals. That's when Indu asked me, "Do you believe in logic or in the magic of the Law of Attraction?" Obviously my answer was, "I believe in the magic of the Law of Attraction."

"Then let's apply the golden rule of not asking how. Just manifest, just believe that it's done and then the universal energy will create the conditions required to give us what we want," she said.

I thought for a minute and decided that I would start believing that I have already achieved a 50 per cent increase in my financial goal in 2012 and I would not worry about the "How?" I would do my best and stop worrying about the results.

I achieved more than 50 per cent financial growth in 2012 even though my first book was published in November 2013!

This is how we ourselves create unconscious blocks in our feelings, thoughts, beliefs or actions because of which the Law of Attraction does not work for us sometimes.

If you also think you are blocking your frequency somewhere then check all your four elements.

Not taking enough action – If you use visualization, affirmations, gratitude, positive thinking but have not taken enough action to move towards your goals, you block the frequency again.

For example, if you manifest that you have earned a million dollars but just sit at home and don't take any action, you won't get the opportunities to attract the million dollars.

A participant once wanted to achieve the employee of the month award and was manifesting the whole month but instead of him, someone else got the employee of the month award. He was quite angry and told me that the Law of Attraction was futile.

I asked him to calm down and tell me honestly how much action he had taken to deserve the employee of the month award compared to his colleague who actually got the award?

After some resistance he accepted that he had not been as proactive at work as his colleague had been. He realized that he felt, thought, and believed that he had got the award but he had not acted like an employee of the month.

He understood this and aligned his actions with his feelings, thoughts and beliefs and the next month he received the employee of the month award.

The best part was that he was not surprised when he got the award because he said he had lived it the entire month.

Remember that your frequency-tuning requires alignment of all your feelings, thoughts, beliefs and actions as well. If you find yourself stuck at the action level go back to Chapter 11 on Actions and re-learn it.

Negative talk – Negative talking creates negative frequency which also blocks the right frequency.

If you want to attract great business but constantly talk negatively about the market situation, you won't attract the opportunities that exist out there.

On the contrary, because of the negative talking, you will attract the negative frequency of challenges and problems which also exist in the market.

Be conscious of saying anything negative about your goals. Say 'Cancel-Cancel' to remove that frequency and replace it with a positive affirmation to tune into the right frequency.

Less gratitude, more complaints – This is one of the most hidden and dangerous ways of blocking the frequency of your goals. Be conscious if you are complaining and cribbing about what you have. Stop it immediately and replace it with gratitude for what you already have.

The more you focus on being grateful for what you have, the more you will get to be grateful for. The more you complain about what you don't have, the more you will get to complain for.

Attached, not committed – There is a difference between attachment and commitment of which most people are unaware.

Attachment has emotions like insecurity, jealousy, doubt, etc. Attachment means you won't accept failure while commitment involves emotions like security, confidence, trust, etc. because commitment implies that you are committed to make it happen irrespective of what happens along the way.

If you are attached to your goals you create negative emotional frequency, so drop the attachment. This doesn't mean you let go of your goal; stay committed but not attached. Attachment will only block your positive frequency.

Here is what I do when I am too attached to something. For example, I was once too attached to my goal of making my book a bestseller and this was blocking my positive frequency.

So I kept my right hand on my heart, closed my eyes and said that my book has to be a bestseller, I wouldn't accept it any other way. The negative emotion of attachment was strong. I continued to keep my eyes shut, my right hand on my heart and said that it is fine if my book is not a bestseller, my life does not depend on it.

Surprisingly, I felt light hearted, as if a burden had been taken off my chest. Then I closed my eyes again and visualized that my book is already a bestseller and that I am in a temple thanking God for the success of my book.

This time I was able to manifest without any fear because I had dropped the attachment of success, I was no longer afraid of failing.

While these can be some of the reasons why LOA may not work for you at times, here is one of the most important reasons.

Destiny

One of the reasons why you may not be attracting what you want despite all your efforts is probably because you are not destined for it.

How do we know whether we are destined for something or not?
Well, actually there is no real answer for this question. No one really knows whether you are destined for something or not.

So then how do I know whether I will attract what I want?
You don't.

So should I give up on my goal or keep working on it?
Only your heart can answer this question but allow me to explain what I mean with a small story.

When Thomas Edison was inventing the electric bulb, he failed a thousand times before he succeeded. Did he have the guarantee that he would succeed? No. So why did he not give up even after failing a thousand times?

Because he had unconditional love for what he was doing; whether he succeeded or failed, he would keep doing it until he died. There was no condition in his commitment to his goal; that's unconditional love.

So if you asked him how long he would keep trying before he succeeded, I'm sure his answer would be as long as it takes. That's the power of unconditional love. When we are in love with someone or something, we don't leave it at any cost.

For example, when a child learns to walk, he falls a thousand times but the parents never give up. They keep supporting the child and helping the child until he succeeds because they have unconditional love for their child.

Ask yourself, do you have unconditional love for your goal? Are you willing to keep working on it forever? If the answer is positive, you must keep working on it whether you are destined for it or not.

Human beings are the only living beings who have the ability to consciously create their own destiny. So be the director of your own life and the designer of your own destiny.

Success and failure is not important when you have unconditional love.

At the same time, if you give up in the face of problems and don't have the persistence to continue working on your goals, then you know that it is not meant for you because you don't have the unconditional love required for that goal or person.

Once my mentor told me a great story that helped me a great deal to understand destiny.

It's not a true story but it's a very powerful story that has always guided my decisions. Here I share the same story with you hoping it will serve you the way it has always served me.

When we were not born, when we were in our pure form of energy, when we were God, we could not see all that we could do or be. In our pure form of energy, when we were God, we decided to take birth as human beings to experience life in many forms.

Part of our energy chose to become rich and find out how it feels to be rich. Part of our energy chose to become poor and find out how it feels to be poor and become rich by taking control of our life. Part of our energy chose to become a man, part of our energy chose to be a woman and this way we chose many forms to experience all aspects of life on earth.

It is like going to the movies to experience happiness, sadness, fear, excitement, pain, joy, humour, etc. through a variety of films. We chose different forms of life to experience everything but it would be boring if we knew everything about what we would experience, just like it would be boring to know the story of a movie before we watch it.

So we decided that 20 per cent of our experience would be chosen by us as our destiny but 80 per cent of our life would depend on how we live our life, what choices we make, at what energy we vibrate.

So a part of our life was chosen by us as our destiny and to keep it interesting, part of it was left to how we play the game of life. The interesting part is that we ourselves chose our destiny before we came to earth in our present life form.

We chose our parents; we chose whether we wanted to experience an easy life or a difficult life. We chose all kinds of experiences in our destiny like love, sadness, happiness, betrayal, fear, success, triumph, failure, action, comedy, almost everything just as in a complete movie.

But again, my mentor repeated, we chose our own destiny before we took birth in this form. So even our destiny is our choice; what we do in this life, what we attract is also our choice, so our entire life is our choice.

You are never a victim of your life; you are the creator of your life, including the 20 per cent destiny and the 80 per cent choices you make in this lifetime.

I was quite fascinated by this powerful story by which to live our life. Then my mentor said something that summarised the entire story for me in just two sentences; it has had a great positive influence on me.

You are not a human being who came to this earth to experience being spiritual.
You are already a spiritual being who came to this earth to experience being human.

I hope this chapter has helped you understand why the Law of Attraction may not work at times and how you can change that.

Now let's get into details of how we can use the Law of Attraction for every area of our life.

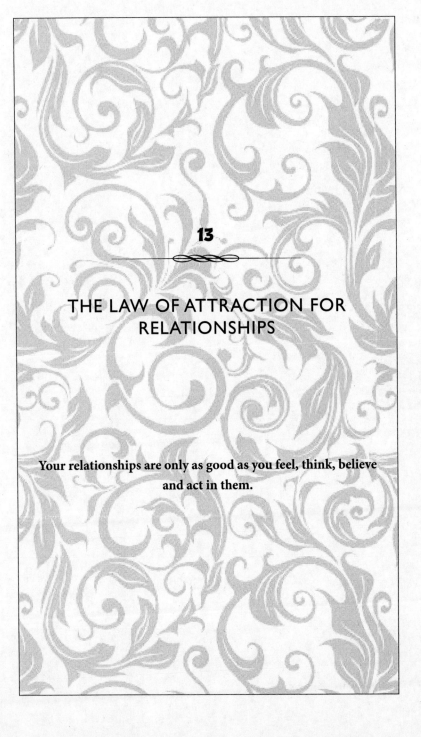

13

❧

THE LAW OF ATTRACTION FOR RELATIONSHIPS

Your relationships are only as good as you feel, think, believe and act in them.

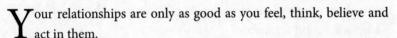

Your relationships are only as good as you feel, think, believe and act in them.

Relationships are made of people; people are made of material body, which is made of energy. You and others are made of the same energy and thus we are all connected at the level of energy.

Every person has potential negative and positive energy within them. When you have negative FTBAs about them, you attract their negative energy towards you. As a result, they also feel, think, believe and act negatively about you.

At one time, my wife Indu did not have a good relationship with my mother. She realized that she could not change how her mother-in-law behaved with her unless she changed her own frequency.

She realized that she was conditioned with the traditional belief that it is not possible for mothers-in-law to have a good relationship with their daughters-in-law. This is a common belief and most people don't question it.

Indu decide to change her frequency by feeling, thinking, believing and acting positively towards her mother-in-law. She used her favourite technique, the Ho Opno-Opno.

This is a technique where you say four statements which have very high positive frequency while thinking of a particular person. As a result, you start tuning into a very high positive frequency towards them.

These four statements are:

- I love You
- Thank You
- Please forgive me
- I am sorry

All Indu did was say these four statements while thinking of her mother-in-law a few times each day. As a result, in just a couple of days my mother called her and made an effort to improve their relationship. She even got a gift for Indu!

This happened in only two days after Indu started using the Ho Opno Opno technique to feel, think, believe and act positively towards Mom.

You got to be aware of your FTBAs with all your relationships. If you are constantly upset, cribbing, believing that things will never change and act half-heartedly in a relationship, you will keep attracting negative energy.

A participant once asked me, "How can I think positively about my boss when he keeps irritating me?" My answer is, if you really want to change your boss's behaviour towards you, you must start using positive feelings, thoughts, beliefs and actions towards him even if he is being negative.

The question is not how to be positive but whether you understand the importance of being positive. Because if you understand the importance then you know that having positive thoughts in a negative situation can magically attract positive results for you.

Here is a simple exercise to practice the Law of Attraction for relationships.

Write your current FTBAs in your relationships:

Relationships	Feelings	Thoughts	Beliefs	Actions
Parents				
Friends				
Life partner				
Colleagues				
Children				

After you have recognized your current frequency of FTBAs choose your new frequency of FTBAs here:

Relationships	Feelings	Thoughts	Beliefs	Actions
Parents				
Friends				
Life partner				
Colleagues				

In order to condition this new frequency of FTBAs:

- Use the visualization technique right now for each of these relationships to experience that you already have what you want with them.
- Write down your affirmations right now to condition new thoughts based on what you want to attract in this relationship.
- Use the gratitude technique to regularly say thank you for having these relationships exactly the way you want them. Record these affirmations and listen to them at night.

- Check for any limiting beliefs that may be blocking your ability to deserve and attract great relationships. Then use the belief transforming steps to change your limiting beliefs into growing beliefs.
- Finally start taking the required actions to attract what you want. Remember to act as if you already have what you want.

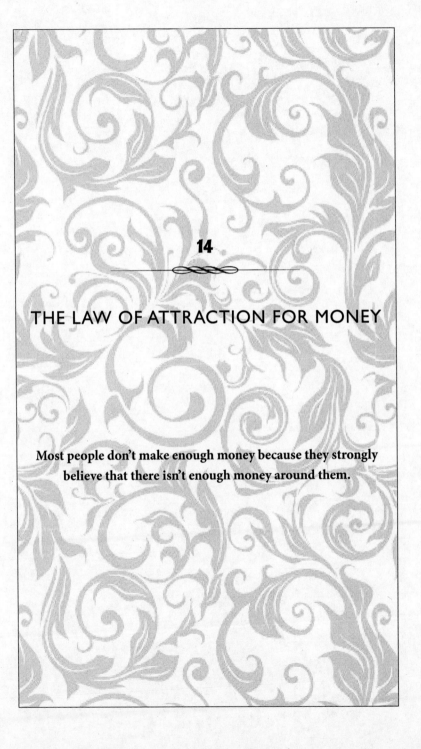

14

THE LAW OF ATTRACTION FOR MONEY

Most people don't make enough money because they strongly
believe that there isn't enough money around them.

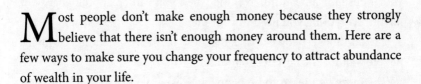

Most people don't make enough money because they strongly believe that there isn't enough money around them. Here are a few ways to make sure you change your frequency to attract abundance of wealth in your life.

Observe What You Want, Not What You Don't Want

The more you observe the lack of money, the more you attract such situations. What do I mean by this?

Like I said many times earlier, positive and negative frequency is always around you. What you observe the most is what you attract the most.

If you constantly observe and acknowledge examples of how people are not doing well in their business, jobs and how the market lacks money, you will vibrate more at that frequency and thus attract the same.

On the other hand, if you consciously observe rich people and use them as references to (not feel jealous) feel sure that there are opportunities to get rich, there are people who are making a lot of money, there are people who are living in abundance, you will vibrate at a 'rich' frequency and thus start attracting the same.

So starting now, you must observe and acknowledge the existence of all those things that you want. FTBA as if you already have them because that's the only way to vibrate at its exact frequency.

Be Happy With What You Have

You always have enough to be happy in life but when you focus on what you don't have, you start vibrating at the frequency of unhappiness.

I am not saying stop thinking of what you want but be happy with what you have first. If you have less money to go out for a party learn to be happy with that little money and create a small economical party at home. Lovely music, homemade food and candle lights can transform your house for a beautiful evening when you can create the energy of having everything you need in your life.

Extraordinary people make the best of their situations; ordinary people wait for the best of situations.

The more you learn to be happy with what you have, the more you will attract happiness in your life. It is simple science; happy people attract happiness!

Here is an exercise to use the Law of Attraction for abundance of money:

FTBAs	Current frequency of money	New frequency of money
Feelings		
Thoughts		
Beliefs		
Actions		

In order to condition this new frequency of FTBAs to attract desired wealth:

- Use the visualization technique right now to see that you have already started making the money you want.
- Write down your affirmations right now to condition new thoughts based on what you want to attract in terms of money.
- Use the gratitude technique to regularly say thank you for the money that you already have and also for the money that is being attracted to you as if you have already got it.
- Check for any limiting beliefs that may be blocking your ability to deserve and attract money. Then use the belief transforming steps to change your limiting beliefs into growing beliefs.
- Finally start taking the required actions to attract what you want. Remember to act as if you already have what you want.

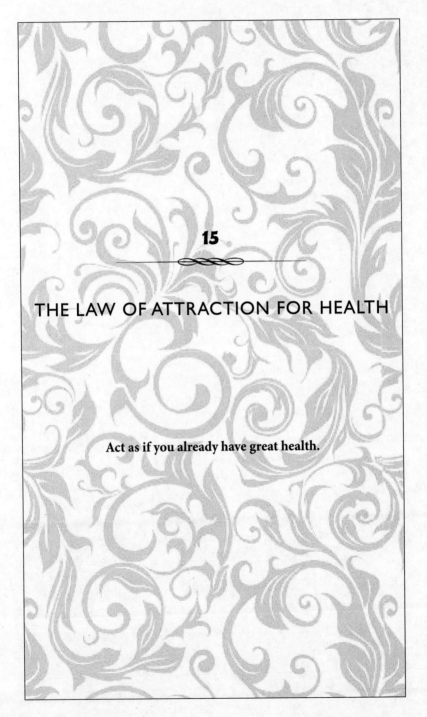

15

THE LAW OF ATTRACTION FOR HEALTH

Act as if you already have great health.

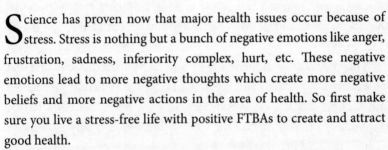

Science has proven now that major health issues occur because of stress. Stress is nothing but a bunch of negative emotions like anger, frustration, sadness, inferiority complex, hurt, etc. These negative emotions lead to more negative thoughts which create more negative beliefs and more negative actions in the area of health. So first make sure you live a stress-free life with positive FTBAs to create and attract good health.

How can someone attract good health? Positive and negative bacteria are always around you. When you have a weak immune system (result of weak FTBAs), you will easily attract negative bacteria that lead to bad health. However, if you have positive FTBAs of health, you will have a strong immune system which will attract the positive bacteria and repel the negative ones. If you already have some health issues then here is what you need to do:

Stop Talking About Your Bad Health To Everyone

Most people who have health issues enjoy talking about it to their friends and relatives. The more they talk about it, the more they reinforce their bad health frequency. So stop talking about it immediately.

When people ask you how you are doing, tell them you are getting better every day. The more you talk positively about your health, the more positive you will feel, think and act and thus you will recover faster.

In fact feel, think, believe and act as if you are already healed and you will be surprised at how rapidly your body starts healing itself.

Have you heard about the Miracle Man? He met with an accident in a plane crash and broke almost every bone in his body. Most importantly, his diaphragm was damaged due to which he needed a machine to help him breathe.

Doctors said he wouldn't recover soon and may never be able to breathe on his own without the help of a machine. The Miracle Man knew about the Law of Attraction and thus also of the power of his own feelings, thoughts, beliefs and actions. So firstly he ignored what the doctors said and decided that he would be out of the hospital by Christmas.

While he was bed ridden in the hospital, he started visualizing that he was already walking and breathing normally. He made sure he felt and thought like he was already healed. As a result, his body started responding and one day he was able to breathe normally once again without the help of a machine.

He even got his strength back to walk out of the hospital by Christmas, exactly as he had decided. You can search YouTube for the Miracle Man and see the video of his miraculous healing.

Here is an exercise to use the Law of Attraction for health:

FTBAs	Current frequency of health	New frequency of health
Feelings		
Thoughts		
Beliefs		
Actions		

In order to condition this new frequency of FTBAs to attract desired wealth:

- Use the visualization technique right now to see that you are already healthy and full of vitality.
- Write down your affirmations right now to create and maintain good health.
- Use the gratitude technique to regularly say thank you for the health that you already have and also for the health that is being attracted to you as if you already have it.
- Check for any limiting beliefs that may be blocking your ability to deserve and attract good health. Then use the belief transforming steps to change your limiting beliefs into growing beliefs.
- Finally, start taking the required actions to attract good health. Remember to act as if you already have what you want.

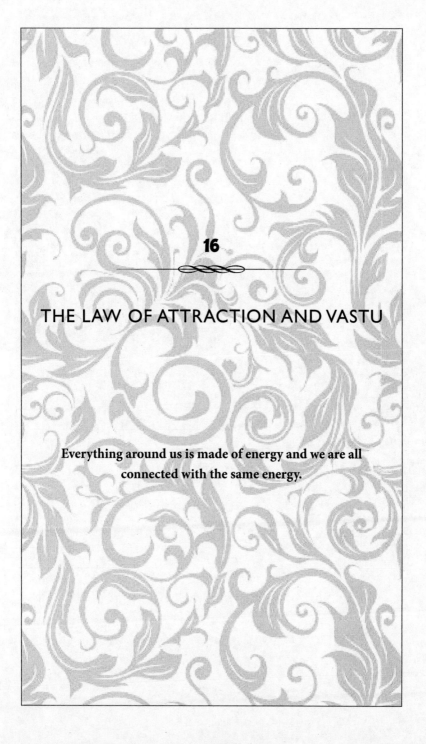

16

THE LAW OF ATTRACTION AND VASTU

Everything around us is made of energy and we are all connected with the same energy.

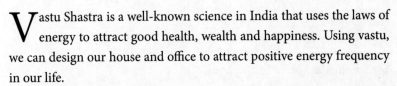

Vastu Shastra is a well-known science in India that uses the laws of energy to attract good health, wealth and happiness. Using vastu, we can design our house and office to attract positive energy frequency in our life.

I did not believe in vastu till I understood its scientific connection with the Law of Attraction.

Remember that everything around us is made of energy and we are all connected with the same energy. So the house we live in or the office we work in also has its own energy which constantly impacts our energy since we live and work in it.

Vastu is the science that helps us understand which direction of our house has positive and negative energy as per the laws of nature. **Here are some basic laws of nature explained in vastu:**

- There are four primary directions: north, south, east and west.
- There are five sub-directions: south-east, north-east, north-west, south-west and centre.
- Each of these five sub-directions is made of five elements of nature: fire, water, air, earth and space.

- Each element has its own energy frequency and thus has a certain impact on us.

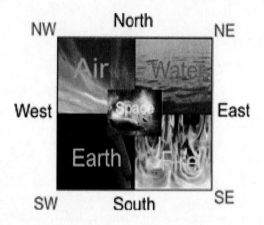

Each element has its own positive and negative frequencies which impact our state of mind and body.

For example, if we sleep facing the right directions as per vastu which is east and north we will get positive energy which will give us a great state of mind, body, health, wealth and relationships.

Why? Because when the sun rises in the east, maximum positive energy from the sun comes in from the east and north.

If we sleep facing the wrong direction, west and south as per vastu, then the negative energy of that direction will impact our state of mind and body negatively.

Why? Because west and south are directions where the cosmic energy is draining. So it is important that we don't sleep facing south and west.

The earth has electromagnetic waves which impact us from every direction. Vastu is the science that explains which direction of your house is best for a particular task. Here are some ideal vastu points:

If you look at the above vastu directions picture, south-east is the zone of fire element. So obviously all fire related tasks like cooking should be done here. Thus the ideal place for a kitchen in any house is the south-east zone. And since east is where the positive cosmic energy comes in from, it is best to face east while cooking in the kitchen.

South-west zone is the earth element which means it is a zone with very stable and powerful energy. Thus the master bedroom is best in the south-west zone of any house. Scientifically if you sleep in the south-west zone you will be sleeping in highly stable energy all night which will help you remain stable and powerful in your state of mind when you work during the day.

The guest bedroom is best in the north-west zone which is the air element since you want the guests to come and go like air, not stay forever.

The temple is best kept in the north-east area since that is the water element, also known as the zone of God (*Ishanya* in Sanskrit). You must face east or north while praying.

Vastu is a deep science and it is practically impossible to do justice to it in one chapter. I would have to write a complete book on it. The intention here is simply to help you understand the seriousness and importance of vastu. The house you are living in, the office you are working in plays a big role in your life and thus you must pay attention to them.

Energy coming from certain directions impacts you in certain ways. So you must learn about the laws of energy hidden in the laws of vastu.

When I did the vastu analysis of my old house, this is what the vastu consultant said simply by looking at the map of my house:

- Your wife has regular headaches (migraine problem).
- You make a lot of money but you end up spending so much that you always seem to be short of money.
- You start a project with a lot of enthusiasm but lose interest half the way.
- You travel very frequently.

I have a lot of respect for Nirmal Shah, a vastu expert from Pune. He is truly one of the best human beings I have met in my life. I was quite shocked about how Nirmal made such accurate predictions about my life based only on the map of my house.

This is when I started researching more about vastu and realized that it is completely based on the study of the Law of Attraction.

So I did a certification on vastu with Nirmal (deep gratitude to him for that) and became a vastu student myself. I made specific changes in my house based on vastu and saw the positive results immediately

During my vastu lessons, I learnt that in life:

- Twenty five per cent is based on past life actions.
- Twenty five per cent is based on our feelings, thoughts and beliefs.
- Twenty five per cent is based on our actions (karma).
- Twenty five per cent is based on our vastu.

Now we cannot do anything about our past life. Most people never take control of their feelings, thoughts, beliefs and actions. Neither do they take control of their house vastu. As a result, a lot of people unconsciously attract negative energy.

The intention of this book is to inspire you to take control of the 75 per cent of your life – 25 per cent of your feelings and thoughts, 25 per cent of your actions and also the 25 per cent of the vastu of your home and workplace.

Unfortunately, it is not possible to cover the complete scope of vastu in this book or I would have. What you can do is find a vastu consultant in your area and get your house and office vastu analyzed and make the required corrections.

Vastu – An Amazing Fact

We attract a house based on our current energy frequencies. So a person with positive energy will naturally attract a house with all the right vastu directions in place while a person with negative energy will attract a house with all the wrong vastu directions.

You can consciously change your external environment with the help of vastu which will eventually impact your internal energy and help you attract positive things in your life.

Hope this motivates you to learn more about vastu and its connection with the Law of Attraction so you immediately take control of it.

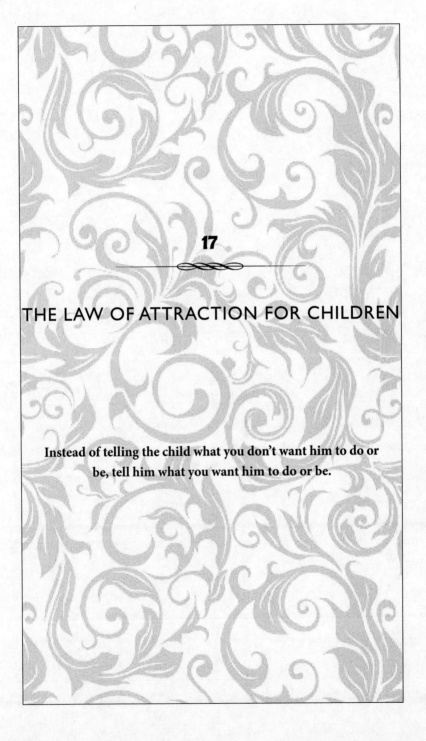

17

THE LAW OF ATTRACTION FOR CHILDREN

Instead of telling the child what you don't want him to do or
be, tell him what you want him to do or be.

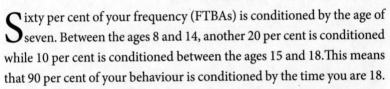

Sixty per cent of your frequency (FTBAs) is conditioned by the age of seven. Between the ages 8 and 14, another 20 per cent is conditioned while 10 per cent is conditioned between the ages 15 and 18. This means that 90 per cent of your behaviour is conditioned by the time you are 18.

After that you are like a conditioned radio attracting more or less the same frequency all your life, unless you learn to take control of your conditionings, your frequency and your FTBAs.

The techniques discussed in this book give you the opportunity and guidelines to change your frequency to attract what you want and less of what you don't want.

But imagine the power of learning all this at the age of 7 or 14 or 16! Wouldn't it be amazing to learn to control our own frequency since childhood?

Well you cannot go back in age but you can give this privilege to your children.

There are two ways in which you can do this:

- Condition them to have a positive frequency using the Law of Attraction techniques.
- Teach them LOA so they can control their own frequency.

Do you know that unknowingly you condition your children for negative frequency? Well, most people do since they don't understand the power of conditioning and the Law of Attraction.

Consider what we tell our children:

- You are a bad boy/girl.
- You never listen to me.
- You have become a rebel.
- You are bad at sports.
- You are bad at math.
- You don't have manners.
- You always keep your room untidy.

There are many negative things that we say to our children which condition them to have negative feelings, thoughts, beliefs and actions about life, work, relationships, career, money, etc.

So what do we do?

Firstly, recognize a list of all the negative things you say to your children because awareness is the key to change. Then make a list of how to say the same things positively.

Here is a list of examples:

Negative frequency conditioning	Positive frequency conditioning
You are a bad boy/girl.	You are a good boy/girl.
You never listen to me.	You are a good listener.
You have become a rebel.	You are a disciplined child.
You are bad at sports.	You are excellent at sports.
You are bad at math.	You are good at math.

You don't have manners.	You have good manners.
You always keep your room untidy.	You always keep your room clean.

Instead of telling the child what you don't want him to do or be, tell him what you want him to do or be.

Convert all your negative commands into positive commands.

Next get them to practice some Law of Attraction techniques like saying "Cancel-Cancel" when they say something negative like, "I am not interested in studies". Ask them to say something positive like, "Studying is easy and fun".

Help them make their own affirmations and make sure they say them loudly to you every day when they get up in the morning and every day before they sleep at night.

Get them used to saying thanks for everything in life.

Be aware that you help them create positive and growing beliefs for every area of their life.

The more you teach children to practice the Law of Attraction at an earlier age, the better they are able to control what they attract in their life while they grow up.

With this chapter coming to an end we have also come to the end of this book but I want you to know that the Law of Attraction is a lifelong practice, so the journey doesn't end here, it continues.

So all the best and I would love to receive an email from you and learn about the miracles you create as you practice the Law of Attraction, your personal genie!

All the best!

I hope I have been able to serve you through this book to attract your dreams and live a successful and happy life.

It would be great if you add a review for this book online, it would help spread the word about it to many more people.

Thank You!

RECAP

Knowledge becomes wisdom only when we implement it.

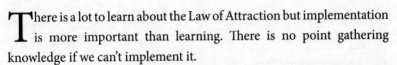

There is a lot to learn about the Law of Attraction but implementation is more important than learning. There is no point gathering knowledge if we can't implement it.

While you have reached the end of this book, you have just begun the journey of becoming a master practitioner of the Law of Attraction. So I want to conclude by giving you a recap of everything we have learnt so that you can access everything in one place.

In this chapter, I have divided the entire book into two parts: theory and practical techniques. The theory helps us to understand the Law of Attraction and the practical techniques section helps us to implement and practice the Law of Attraction so that we use its magic to attract our desired life and achieve our goals. To make it interesting, I have presented the recap in the form of a fill in the blanks test, so use a pencil to fill it up.

Here we go…

Theory

1. The Law of Attraction is like a _____ that can help you attract whatever you want in your life.

2. We all have a personal genie that is hidden _____ us.

3. Yesterday's _____ is today's science and today's magic is tomorrow's _____.

4. This science of the Law of Attraction was revealed by Lord _____ centuries ago in _____.

5. We learnt about the Law of Attraction in school in _____ subject.

6. In physics, we learnt that everything is matter and all that is matter is made of _____.

7. We are all made of the same _____ and we are all connected, we are _____.

8. The only difference between us is in the _____ at which we vibrate.

9. The total amount of _____ in the universe is always _____.

10. Energy cannot be _____ nor destroyed, it can only be transformed from one form to another.

11. Energy is always _____ at a certain frequency.

12. There is only one infinite source of energy that we are all made of, only the _____ of energy is different.

13. All matter is made of the same _____.

14. Energy with the same frequency will _____ each other which means like _____ like.

15. 'Like attracts like' means energy with the same _____ will _____ each other.

16. There are only two types of energy frequencies in the world which we can attract: _____ or high energy frequency and _____ or low energy frequency.

17. It is your own _____ which is attracting negative or positive situations and people in your life.

18. 'Like attracts like' and 'opposites attract' really mean energetic _____.

19. If you learn to _____ at the exact _____ of your goals then it is logical that you shall attract it because like attracts like.

20. We must learn to control our _____ so that we can control what we _____.

21. Our energy frequency is made of four elements our _____, _____, _____ and _____.

22. The way to vibrate at the exact frequency of your goals is to feel, think, believe and act (FTBA) as if you _____.

23. You can change your attractions only by changing your _____ frequency.

24. Ordinary people let their situations define their FTBAs while extraordinary people use their _____ to define their situations.

Practical Techniques

Now let's recap the practical techniques to implement and practice the Law of Attraction.

1. Change your frequency by changing your feelings, thoughts, beliefs and actions.

2. Visualization technique – you attract what you imagine.

3. Gratitude technique – a shortcut to all positive attractions.

4. Use conscious positive questions to create positive emotional energy before unconscious negative questions create negative emotional energy.

5. You can also control the flow of your emotional energy by controlling the flow of what you talk.

6. Practice forgiveness and acceptance to release the hand brakes of positive emotional energy.

7. Use affirmations to tune your thought frequency.

8. Record affirmations to program your subconscious mind.

9. Feed yourself with great thoughts.
10. Change your limiting beliefs into growing beliefs.
11. To attract what you want, you must increase your deserving capacity by converting your limiting beliefs into growing beliefs.
12. To attract massive results you must take massive action.
13. Add positive value through your actions to attract positive results
14. Take action as if you already have it.
15. Don't ask "how?"
16. Live in the perfect zone.
17. Collect positive references that the Law of Attraction works.
18. Practice unconditional happiness instead of unconditional sadness.
19. Meet LOA practitioners to get support in applying the Law of Attraction.
20. Coaching is a faster way to learn and practice LOA from someone else's experience.
21. Stop using LOA when required.

Hope the above recap of theory and practical techniques will help you to practice and implement the Law of Attraction to attract your goals. Remember,

**Destiny makes decisions for the weak ones,
strong ones get to make their own destiny.**

I hope this book has been of service and value for you. Thank you for reading till the end, I look forward to hearing some of your success stories.